Habits of the Soul

Learning to Live on Purpose

HABITS
OF THE
Soul

Learning to Live on Purpose

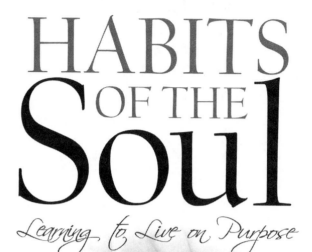

LINDA PERRONE ROONEY

Dedication

For Joe,
a man of prayer
who prays for me, even now

The Scripture passages contained herein are from the *New Revised Standard Version of the Bible*, ©1989, by the Division of Christian Education of the National Council of Churches of Christ in the U.S.A. Used by permission. All rights reserved.

Twenty-Third Publications
A Division of Bayard
One Montauk Avenue, Suite 200
New London, CT 06320
(860) 437-3012 or (800) 321-0411
www.23rdpublications.com
ISBN 10: 1-58595-554-X
ISBN 978-1-58595-554-1

Library of Congress Catalogue Card Number: 2005935302
Printed in the U.S.A.

Contents

Habits of the Soul: Learning to Live On Purpose

Now is the acceptable time. 2 CORINTHIANS 6:2

›› INTRODUCTION

The next forty days will mirror the forty days that Jesus spent in the desert preparing to undertake his mission. They are a time to pause in your busy life and turn your heart to God. Whether you are starting this journey as a lenten exercise, or simply because the Holy Spirit has directed you to your need for spiritual renewal, now is the "acceptable time" to examine your life. It's a time to slow down, to take time each day to pray, to reflect, and to understand more deeply what it is the Lord wants of you.

These forty days are an opportunity to make changes; to create new habits of the soul. It is a time to really live, to do so on purpose and to keep your eye on the purpose of life.

Living on purpose means staying on course. It means deciding to deepen your spiritual life. And here's the reward: At the end of

1

these days you will have a more peaceful heart, deeper spiritual well-being, and a clearer sense of the purpose for your life.

So, I invite you to really live during the next forty days. But be forewarned: It will not be easy. The journey to the heart of the Lord is never made without effort. The process of living on purpose asks you to commit yourself to one half-hour, each day, for forty days. During this half-hour, you are invited to be quiet and still, to hold this book in your hands and use the exercises here to lead you to a profound encounter with Christ.

If you're ready for this focus in your life, then *Habits of the Soul: Learning to Live on Purpose* comes at the right moment for you. Can you be committed to this process? Will you give yourself to it completely? Are you ready to offer this daily half-hour? If so, witness to your commitment by signing the covenant below, and let's get started.

My Covenant

Fully believing that I am a blessed child of God, I will walk a path of renewal through these forty days, endeavoring to create new and healthy habits of the soul.

I will strive to live on purpose, with conviction and trust that my efforts will blossom into lifelong practice.

I will take the time to look deeply into my heart and soul, honestly examining the patterns and behaviors that keep me from holy living and obscure my vision of God.

I will pray and commit myself to good works, guided by the principles of Christian living.

I will develop ways to live as a true disciple of Jesus Christ, faithful to my baptismal call and ever ready to further the kingdom of God in our midst.

May my life become a living sign of the goodness of God, and a constant reflection of God's word.

Signed, _____

Needed: Open Heart Surgery

>> INTRODUCTION

You've crossed a threshold. You've acknowledged a desire for God and have now committed to honor this desire and to seek God where God may be found.

Today, you examine your heart, your motives, your ability to acquire healthy habits of the soul that enable you to do that which God places in your heart to do.

Today, you take the first step toward living your life on purpose. It is exciting. Hand in hand with Christ you can do all things.

>> SCRIPTURE

So we are ambassadors for Christ, since God is making his appeal through us; we entreat you on behalf of Christ, be reconciled to God.
2 CORINTHIANS 5:20

Even now, says the Lord, return to me with all your heart, with fasting, with weeping, and with mourning; rend your hearts and not your clothing. JOEL 2:12

>> Reflection

If your heart becomes weakened and disabled, unable to be a source of life, vitality, and energy for the rest of your body, the quality of your life suffers. If you fail to change your eating and exercise habits, or do nothing to improve the quality of your heart's ability to function, then the likelihood of dying sooner than expected increases significantly.

Most people, when faced with leading a debilitated life, will do everything they can to heal their hearts and to improve their chances at living a long life. They carve out a daily routine that includes three low-fat, nutritious meals, thirty to sixty minutes of exercise, research, or reading that helps them understand their illness and the factors contributing to it, the proper amount of rest and sleep, low-stress relationships, and the like. They are conscious every day that their lives could be harmed if they do not maintain this discipline. They value their lives so much that they make the necessary sacrifices. They stop and smell the flowers.

>> Return to the Lord

This first day of your journey to living on purpose,
    reminds you that your spiritual check-up
    is not something that can be done just once
        and then forgotten.
Joel, the prophet, speaks for God when he says,
    "Return to me with all your heart...
    return to the Lord for he is gracious and merciful,
    slow to anger,
    and abounding in steadfast love,
    and relents from punishing." (Joel 2:12–13)
Joel seems to assume that you have turned away from God,
    that somehow, your heart is not fully engaged
    with the one who created you
    and whose love gives you life into each new day.

But how do you return to the Lord,
    especially if you are frightened by what you see
    when you look into your heart?
How do you return to the Lord
    if it has been a long time,
    or if, when you were away,
    you abandoned what you knew would please God?
How do you summon the courage to face the One
    whom you think you have disappointed?
How do you return to one you may never have known?
There are five steps to take
    and in these first days of your renewal
    we will take them together,
        one by one.
Today, you take the first tentative step
    and begin to *live on purpose* once again.

›› Step One

Make an act of the will. Returning to God with your whole heart requires a deliberate act of the will. You must make a choice, plain and simple. It's a choice that needs to be made daily. The daily rising of the sun is a sign of God's renewed covenant of love with all humanity. Each day, God remembers how much love God has for all of creation. This remembering moves God to sustain life for another day. Your desire to return to God is shown by daily turning to God in prayer, in getting up each day to renew your covenant to seek and find God that day.

›› Help With Step One

Reflect on the questions that follow. Your answers will help you change your habits and live your desire to put God first.

- Where will I try to be still and quiet each day?
- What time of day is best for my prayer? When will I be least distracted and have the most time to give?

- What fears or anxieties might keep me from meeting with God in prayer each day?
- Who is someone I could ask to be a companion on this journey, prodding me when I want to quit or reminding me of my commitment?
- When will I contact this companion and ask for their help?
- Do I need to get any of the tools that might help me during these forty days:
  —a Bible
  —a notebook for thoughts that may not fit in this book
  —a candle to help me remember this is sacred time?

›› REFLECTION/JOURNAL WRITING

Your Father knows what you need before you ask him. MATTHEW 6:8
Pause now to reflect on your decision to use these forty days wisely, as a time to answer God's call to change your heart and fill it with divine love. On a separate piece of paper, write a letter to God describing what you need in order to make God your primary focus for the rest of today.

›› ACTION

Make a decision to notice those who need your heart's compassion today. Perhaps it will be a family member who needs a warm embrace, a coworker in need of affirmation, a stranger in need of a smile or kind word or act. Open your heart to the ways in which God will come to you today, and serve God in that other person.

›› CLOSING PRAYER

O God, you are my source of life, my hope, my healer. It is you who created me and fashioned my heart. It is you who waits patiently for me to hear your voice, to feel your touch and recognize your loving presence. Amen.

What Is Your Heart's Desire?

>> INTRODUCTION

Today is the second day of your covenant. How is it going? Did you meet God yesterday? Coming back to your prayer time today shows that you are really trying to keep your covenant and that you have been successful with step one: an act of the will. Today, you'll work on step two, but let's do some reflecting first.

>> SCRIPTURE

Be reconciled to God. 2 CORINTHIANS 5:20

>> REFLECTION

Everyone struggles to know God's will. Following God's way may seem more difficult than you can manage. You hear about the cross and self-denial, about keeping the commandments and God's laws and feel unsure, maybe even rebellious. You make being God's friend and disciple harder than it really is.

Each day you have the opportunity to make choices that increase or decrease your ability to know and love God. Each choice brings an increase of peace, joy, and energy to live the spiritual life on purpose; or, feelings of discouragement, frustration, and ambivalence toward all that connects you to God. Choices that lead you to a more satisfied life of thanksgiving and praise flow from a receptive heart that has room for God's spirit. Choices that lead to a life of grumbling, dissatisfaction, and anger are the product of a closed heart, one unable to receive all that God wants to give.

God has set before you all that you need to be happy. It does not consist in money, in more objects, or in a surplus of "stuff" to fill every empty space. Rather, it is found in seeing the value in each person, in honoring your relationships and healing broken ones. The happiness that comes from God leads to understanding life as a gift for which you are grateful. It leads you to look at people as gifts that God gives you to lead you deeper into divine life.

>> Return to the Lord

Spiritual renewal demands our attention.
It sounds its inner warning sirens,
    and zeros in on the one thing you want to keep private:
        your relationship with God.
The Spirit calls out,
"Hey, life's not about you or your individual cares or happiness.
It isn't about being so self-absorbed
    that you cannot render compassion to others.
Life is about God and how well you are doing
    as God's son or daughter,
        how well you are carrying out
            God's mission in this world."
In the quiet glow of these forty days,
    you have an opportunity
        to return to God
        to seek out the lost part of you
            that needs a loving embrace
        to offer the broken areas of your life
            to the only One who can heal them

to ask for forgiveness and receive it
to give forgiveness to those who ask.
During these days of covenant,
striving to keep your sacred agreement with God,
you can express your sorrow
and feel the weight of the world
lifted.

›› Step Two

Repent. The second step to the habit of living on purpose is to say you're sorry for being away from God. It means you must be willing to ask for mercy and forgiveness for anything you have done that did not please God. This step may involve pain or fear as you let go of those things that have occupied your heart until now. It may feel uncomfortable and awkward to admit that God has not been your priority. But repentance is the only way to clear the space needed for God to enter. Like the child who "runs away" only to return home hoping for a fresh start and a loving welcome, the first words are, "I'm sorry. May I come home?" Of course, God's answer is always, "Yes, I've been waiting for you."

›› Help with Step Two

Make two lists. One will include anyone you think you may need to apologize to or ask forgiveness of. The second will include anyone who may need your forgiveness. These names could be family members, colleagues at work, neighbors, friends, or anyone with whom you have a broken or tense relationship.

›› Reflection/Journal Writing

Be reconciled to God. 2 Corinthians 5:20
Pause now to reflect on what needs to change in your attitude so that you can see the experiences of your life as a blessing rather than as a curse; as an opportunity to forgive and be forgiven. If you like, you can jot down your thoughts in the space that follows.

_____

_____

_____

_____

_____

›› Action

Make a decision today to do two things:

1. Examine one of your broken relationships to find where you may have failed and honestly admit to God your need to repent.
2. Looking at your two lists, choose one person to contact today and say the words, "I'm sorry," or, "You are forgiven." Each day, look at your lists and choose one more person until your lists are wiped clean.

›› Closing Prayer

Forgiving God, I want to be more fully formed in your ways. I want to pray, fast, forgive, and serve, not because others will see me, but because it pleases you and builds our relationship. Teach me to have a forgiving heart. Amen.

Rend Your Hearts, Not Your Clothing

›› INTRODUCTION

For three days you have chosen to come to this quiet place and pursue your sacred agreement with God. Yesterday, you pushed the boundaries of your heart to include those who you might need to forgive and to seek those who may need to forgive you. Today, you will look at what may be keeping you from creating an open and empty space within that can only be filled by God's love and compassion.

›› SCRIPTURE

Return to me...with fasting. JOEL 2:12

›› REFLECTION

Our culture is full of ads in newspapers and magazines, on TV and the Internet, announcing the next great weight loss gimmick. Advertisers spend millions of dollars each year to sell you products, experiences, and books that will make you slimmer, firmer, and younger, implying that you will then be more prosperous and intelligent, happier and more peaceful. They succeed in their attempts because so many look into the mirror, a metaphor for life, and are disappointed with what they see. Many see unfulfilled dreams, a wasted youth, increased closeness to death, a lack of deep relationships. Some look briefly because it is too painful to admit that their lives are not on track. They don't know what to do; the cost seems too great. Instead of doing the kind of heart-fasting and re-balancing that will lead to the life they want, they spend money on powders, creams, surgery, and acquisitions hoping to fill the void in their hearts; a void that will only be filled when they turn their lives around and re-prioritize their values, relationships, and goals. What do you see when you look in the mirror?

›› What Is the Fast We Need?

There are those who think
    that fasting from what they want
        is mind over matter.
They think they can control
    unhealthy and insecure lives
    with a little positive self-talk.
They crave better lives
    but not the sacrifices that create them.
They want clearer thoughts,
    more meaningful relationships,
    more sincere living;
        but they don't want to suffer in the process.
They won't ever get what they truly want.

The fast God asks is
    heart-rending.
God wants you to
    break open your heart,
    spilling out all those people and things
        that leave no room for God

that distract you from what is good,
healthy,
giving,
compassionate.
God does not want a food fast
or a drink fast
or a fast from good times.
God wants
your undivided attention
your contrition and repentance
center-place in your heart
top of the list in your priorities.
God isn't interested in being in your top ten;
God wants to be Number One.
And for that to happen
you've got to fast from everything else
that clamors for that spot.

›› STEP THREE

Carve out time. Fast from television, cell phone chatter, shopping, and endless driving and give God thirty minutes of living on purpose. Choose a time each day that you will give exclusively to building your relationship with God. Like the heart patients who obsessively include exercise in their health-care regimens, including this spiritual exercise in each day will strengthen your ability to experience God's presence, hear God's voice, and be led by God's will.

Today, renew your commitment to quiet time with this book as your guide. Follow it up with prayers for others as you carpool to work, or loving thoughts of someone you find difficult as you go about your day. Fasting from those things that keep God at a distance will leave room for God to draw closer. Honor the time you are offering God as you would time with a treasured friend. You would not think of disappointing a friend with whom you have made an appointment to spend time. Give God at least as much.

›› Help with Step Three

Here is a calendar. Fill in your appointments with God for each day.

›› Reflection/Journal Writing

Now is the acceptable time; see, now is the day of salvation.
2 Corinthians 6:2

Sit quietly for the next five minutes, focusing on the repeated internal phrase "God fills my emptiness with love." When you are finished, write for another five minutes whatever the Spirit places in your heart.

_____

_____

_____

_____

_____

_____

›› Action

Fasting has a long tradition. It is an act that declares that we rely on God, not on ourselves. In addition to a fast of time for prayer and reflection, choose another offering of time and use it as a way of helping someone else. If you give up television or computer time, consider using it to volunteer with the elderly, or assist someone in your neighborhood, or do some work with children. Today, create a new habit of the soul, then take time and use it to carry out God's mission.

›› Closing Prayer

Claim my heart, O God; empty it of all that is not of you and your mission. Fill me with your wisdom, generosity, and grace. Amen.

Ready, Set, Go

>> INTRODUCTION

With each day since you signed your covenant you have moved steadily toward entering the fullness of renewal and living on purpose. You've made a daily act of the will to set time aside to spend with God in prayer and reflection; to repent for past distractions and sins; to ask for and grant forgiveness; to carve out a special time each day that is a sacred appointment with your loving God.

In your prayer today and in living out the final steps of preparation, you will focus on prayer—both how you pray and preparing yourself for a successful time of prayer. Jesus was a man of prayer. He prayed alone, with his friends, and in huge crowds. He used the Hebrew Scriptures as a foundation for his prayer even as his own life became the content for our Christian Scriptures. Jesus lived and prayed on purpose. So today, keep his example close to your heart as you live your prayer life on purpose.

>> SCRIPTURE

Whenever you pray, go into your room and shut the door and pray....
MATTHEW 6:6

>> REFLECTION

At its heart, prayer is a conversation with God. When you pray, you offer God the thoughts of your mind, the feelings of your heart, and the hopes of your soul. God offers you a listening presence that takes all you give and holds it with love and mercy. Because prayer is a conversation, it has two distinct parts, talking and listening. Some people mistakenly think that the person praying does all the talking and God does all the listening. But that isn't the case. In prayer, God needs a chance to talk to you. God gets that chance when you stop talking in order to listen.

The most transforming conversations are those between people who care about and love each other. In those "soul" conversations, each person has enough love and respect for the other to allow the other time to speak, to pour out what fills them. Each conversation brings the two participants closer together, into a more intimate relationship of trust. Prayer is like that. If you spend all of your prayer time complaining, asking for favors, and bargaining in the face of crises, you lose a precious opportunity to come to know God, to build a relationship of trust and intimacy. Without time to listen, God never gets a chance to reveal God's presence and will.

›› LISTEN FOR THE STILL, SMALL VOICE
Ask yourself,
    "What am I to listen for when I pray?"
Listen for the beat of your heart,
    the sigh of your breath.
Listen for the calming of your pulse,
    the easing of your muscles.
Listen for the feeling of gentle-kindness,
    the welcome of a friend.
Listen for the still, small voice within—
    deep within.
A voice that offers peace,
    not condemnation;
    a voice that offers clarity and the desire for contrition.

A voice that offers a future,
    an understanding of the past;
    hope,
        the energy to live on purpose.
Prayer is your time for intimate conversation
    with God.
Listen.

›› Steps Four and Five

Step Four: *Prepare the way.* Buy a Bible, if you need one. Use this book to journal. Invest in a candle. Select a place at home, or at work, in a place of worship, or in the midst of nature where you can focus your time with God. Paying attention to the environment of your meeting will enhance the experience and put you in a frame of mind and spirit to be receptive to God's presence. Your special time set aside each day doesn't remove the possibility of spontaneous prayer, anywhere, anytime. Instead it offers time for deeper conversation.

Step Five: *Make no excuses.* Don't allow yourself excuses for failing to pursue the urging of the Holy Spirit. Write your exclusive prayer time on your calendar or day planner. When you are tempted to stray from your goal of a deeper spiritual life, remind yourself that nothing else that seems so important can bring you eternal life. Making time to know and love God and to allow God to break into your life with love and direction will bring not only eternal life; but also, peace and happiness in this life. What could be more important than that?

›› Help with Steps Four and Five

Today's reflection on prayer emphasizes listening. The exercise below is offered as one way to settle into a better listening mode. It is called "centering," and you achieve it by concentrating on your breathing. Try this exercise at the beginning of each day's prayer.

Sit in a comfortable chair. Keep your legs and arms uncrossed, relaxed and at ease. Close your eyes. Breathe in through your nose, from your abdomen, as you feel your chest rise and your abdomen drawn in. When you can breathe in no further air, hold that breath for a moment or two. Breathe out through your mouth so that you can hear the air gently escape, and feel your chest lower and your abdomen extend. Continue to breathe in this way for two to five minutes. As you are breathing, become aware of the quiet within you, your shoulders relaxing, your mind clearing. When you are finished, pick up your book and begin your day's reflection and prayer.

›› Reflection/Journal Writing

Do not accept the grace of God in vain.... 2 Corinthians 6:1

Today's reflection allows you time to look back on these first four days, your spiritual progress, and those times you have resisted living on purpose. God's grace is generously offered to you each and every day, a thousandfold. Reflect on how well you have responded to that grace and what fruit it is bearing in your life.

›› Action

Your actions today are simple: gather what you need for your prayer space, practice your breathing and centering, and listen.

›› Closing Prayer

Gentle and listening God, turn your ear to me. Attune my heart to your small voice within and fill my whole being with your presence. Amen.

A Covenant of Trust

>> INTRODUCTION

Today you look at the relationship between covenant and trust, between God's faithfulness and your doubt, God's sustaining love and your fear. What does it mean that God wants to make a sacred agreement of love and protection with creation? How do you feel when you know how much you are loved by your Creator? What resolve and desire wells up in your heart when you realize that the God of Eve, Abraham, Sarah, and Noah, the God of Jesus and of Peter has chosen to make a covenant with you, as well?

To develop the habit of living on purpose, you need to come to grips with your ability to make and keep covenants. These sacred agreements are about believing that God is worthy of your trust and that you, too, are trustworthy. You've signed the covenant to develop new habits of living on purpose. Today you begin to understand what that involves.

>> SCRIPTURE

I establish my covenant with you.... GENESIS 9:11

I will remember my covenant that is between me and you and every living creature.... GENESIS 9:15

›› REFLECTION

Can you imagine being on a boat full of animals for forty days and forty nights, floating on a sea of water without any land in sight? Can you visualize the fear and frustration Noah and his family must have felt? Do you think they were seasick from the wave action, the smells, and lack of fresh foods? How about the arguing that inevitably happens when people have to live together in a crowded space under adverse conditions? It was definitely not a pleasure cruise.

Noah was a good man who tried to live according to God's laws, to keep the covenant of his fathers. He probably didn't understand at first why he had to build the boat. Once it started raining, though, he saw the plan. When it didn't stop raining, it seemed as though they couldn't possibly survive. His family was terrified. The animals made more mess than his small crew could keep up with, and there didn't seem to be any end in sight. Noah prayed with his family for safety. He trusted God to protect them and lead them to dry land. And God did. Do these feelings of ambivalence and confusion, when trying to understand and follow God's instructions for life, sound familiar?

›› OLIVE BRANCH

A dove is sent to seek dry land;
      each time it returns without a sign.
Finally, the dove returns
      carrying an olive branch.
A tree branch, leaves;
      Signs of life, miracle of hope.
Because he honored his agreement,
      Noah and his family are rewarded
            with new life in a new land.

Now God's instructions were clear:
　　build a boat, and
　　fill it with animals that will become
　　　　livelihood in a new land.
Bring cuttings from all the plants
　　that will feed you from generation to generation.
After all the doubt, hope;
　　in the midst of fear, an olive branch.
Just when it seemed that God had forgotten,
　　a rainbow of love and faithfulness appeared.

›› Tips On Learning to Trust

- Decide to be vulnerable.
- Risk being disappointed.
- Release control of the outcome.
- Do the right thing whether or not you can see the reward.

　　Noah trusted that obeying God's instructions would save his family. God trusted that Noah was a man who could be counted on to do what was right. How about you? Are you a trusting person, or do you struggle for control? Are you someone who can be counted on to do the right thing? Today is a time to relearn the meaning of trust in God. It's a time to recapture that innocent soul who knew God's love clearly, before the destructive forces of life threatened to blot it out. It is a safe time to be vulnerable with God, who will never disappoint and who always provides an outcome far more wonderful than we can imagine or invent.

›› Reflection/Journal Writing

Believe in the good news. Mark 1:15

The good news is that "the kingdom of God is near" (Mark 1:15), nearer than we can sometimes see. When you are overcome with doubts and fears, do you ever allow the storms of life to blot out the presence of God?

Think about some times when you failed to trust that God would protect you. Next, think about some ways God has protected you from destruction over the years. Then name people God sent to "share your ark" as you searched for new life. Finally, find one word that fills your heart when you think of God's love for you. If you wish, you can write down your thoughts and feelings about God's faithfulness and your response.

_____

_____

_____

_____

_____

_____

›› ACTION
Take an index card or a nice piece of paper about that size and write or print the word TRUST. If you like, decorate the card and/or the word. Use it for the rest of these forty days as a bookmark, accompanying you on your journey to live on purpose.

›› CLOSING PRAYER
Faithful God, your love and protection are so great. Thank you for your faithful love. Thank you for trusting me. I place my life in your hands. Amen.

Endure Suffering with Hope

›› INTRODUCTION

Yesterday you reflected on God's faithfulness and your ability to trust. Today, you continue to break open the Scripture by reflecting on enduring suffering with hope. Suffering comes in all shapes and sizes. What may seem impossible for one person may be easier to cope with for another. For the Christian, hope sees beyond the present moment. It links you to your baptismal immersion in the suffering and death of Christ and points you to both his resurrection and your own. Take a few moments to sit quietly and breathe deeply before continuing your reflection. Ask the Holy Spirit to be with you and to guide your thoughts.

›› SCRIPTURE

He was in the wilderness forty days.... MARK 1:13

And the angels waited on him. MARK 1:13

›› REFLECTION

One only has to see the Mount of Temptation to appreciate the stark, harsh suffering implied in Mark's gospel. The mountain is high, with a sheer wall of ragged cliff. It is not inviting, and it doesn't take much imagination to believe that wild beasts live there and not much else. It overlooks the lush, green region of Galilee that jumps out at you from the desert surrounding it. As a matter of fact, you have to go through this desert in order to get to Galilee from Jerusalem. After Jesus' baptism in the Jordan, Scripture tells us, "the Spirit immediately drove him out into the wilderness" (Mark 1:12). He went from being one with God, exhilarated by God's blessing as "beloved," to being alone, without food or water, at the mercy of the elements and the wild beasts, for forty days and nights. It suddenly becomes crushingly clear that there will be a cost connected to his mission. Only the naïve would think Jesus did not suffer in that wilderness.

As you reflect on your own wilderness journeys, ask yourself: when have I felt abandoned by God? When has my life lacked nourishment, companionship, or clarity of purpose? Today, remember that, like Jesus, you do not face your times of suffering alone.

›› Endure With Hope

One of the sure realities of life is
 you will not escape suffering.
Days or years may pass in a bleak wilderness
 where you yearn for an end
 and cry out for compassion and mercy,
 but all is quiet.
Then, at the very time of crisis,
 when you can bear no more
  angels come to wait on you.
The fog lifts, the phone rings,
 a note, a word, a gesture or smile,
 your darkened soul sees a glimmer of light;
 what was unbearable becomes a foothold of strength.

Hope weaves its way into your heart.
God is alive again;
>   the way forward is clear.

>> THE ART OF ABANDONMENT

Most people want to avoid suffering at all costs. Yet, as you grow
older you realize that life will bring suffering into your path no
matter how fast you run from it. If you have faith, you also learn
that God walks the path with you; no matter the suffering or pain,
you have Someone who protects and guides you. The secret to cap-
italizing on this guidance is the degree to which you can abandon
yourself to God's will.

Here are three ways you can grow in your ability to abandon
yourself to God:

1. Each day, offer yourself, body and soul, to God's will. Actually
   say the words.
2. When the way seems murky or the suffering is intense, thank
   God and express your acceptance.
3. Pray a prayer of trust in God's love, daily, especially when your
   endurance is tested.

>> REFLECTION/JOURNAL WRITING

According to Mark's gospel, Jesus went to the wilderness alone. At
least we are not told that others accompanied him. Often, this may
seem the case in your own suffering; you are alone. And yet, if you
are honest about it, you are never alone. Not only is God present
in both your joy and your suffering, but God sends others into
your midst to care for you and remind you that you have the
strength you need to follow God's will.

Reflect on your own times of wilderness, of pain or suffering,
but do not stop there. Think, too, about those angels who came
and waited on you, those who showed you God's face and spoke to
you with God's voice and touched your life with God's love—even
if, at the time, you missed the importance of their presence. Can

you picture their faces? Did you keep a note they sent? Were you nourished by their words or deeds? Did their laughter or concern give you added strength? Write awhile about the angels in your own wilderness.

_____

_____

_____

_____

_____

_____

›› ACTION

Choose one person from among the angels you've been reflecting on and write a letter expressing how their word, deeds, or presence nourished you. Tell them how they help you to remember God's protection and guidance. Don't forget to mail the letter.

›› CLOSING PRAYER

Good and loving God, I abandon myself to your will. Be with me in good times and bad. Give me a heart free to love you as you deserve. Amen.

Signs of God's Love

>> INTRODUCTION

Have you ever noticed the number of signs that clog our highways and sidewalks? It seems that businesses, government agencies, non-profit organizations, and even ordinary citizens think signs of every size, color, and description are important ways to get their message across. Often, these messages conflict and you have to be a discerning consumer in order to know which ideas to support and which to ignore. God uses signs, too. Only God's message is always consistent and never harmful.

>> SCRIPTURE

I have set my bow in the clouds, and it shall be a sign of the covenant between me and the earth. GENESIS 9:14

>> REFLECTION

From the first moment of creation God's message has been one of love. Love created the cosmos with its planets and stars, the animals and plants, and finally, humankind. Love offered a paradise of peace where all of creation could live in harmony. Love forgave the selfishness of humans and offered another chance at life. Love made a sacred agreement to guide and protect a chosen people. Love sheltered those seeking a home and defended those under attack. Love sent pillars of fire, and tablets of stone, rulers and prophets and kings. Finally, Love came in person, a sign that could never be outdone in generosity.

We look for signs of God's loving presence. For those who know how to see, they are everywhere.

›› SIGNS OF GOD'S LOVE TODAY

God's love notes,
Unending and unconditional
Gentle rain on parched land,
> Birdcalls
> Flowers that appear, as by magic,
>> Where you least expect to see them.
Sunshine after a violent storm.
> Neighbors helping each other
>> To restore devastated homes.
Children laughing,
> Running, innocent, free.
> Friendships that encourage
>> Families that hug.
Animals that snuggle, wet noses and all.
> Waterfalls, rivers, oceans and seas.
God's love notes,
> Compassion, justice, integrity
> Treating each person with dignity.
God's signs of love are everywhere
> Subtle
> Blatant
Always, always, true.

›› Learning to Become More Aware

Noah and family probably weren't aware that the boat was a sign of love until the water rose and destroyed their town. They probably missed the blessing of sharing space with the animals until that dove came back with an olive branch. It's safe to say they took olive branches for granted and not as a special sign of God's love until they hadn't seen land for forty days. Undoubtedly, everyone on that ark had seen a rainbow before. Now, that bow in the sky was a profound sign of God's providential care. Which changed, the signs or the seekers?

Here are a few ways you can increase your ability to be more aware of the signs of God's love:

- Instead of looking at faces, look into eyes and smile.
- Every day, try to find at least three new, beautiful aspects of nature.
- Stay alert to the kind deeds others do for you each day. As soon as you realize one, say thank you. Whenever you say thank you, raise a prayer to God's love.
- Each time you turn on a faucet, flip a light switch, turn a car key, and receive what you seek, thank God's love.
  Can you add to this list?

›› Reflection/Journal Writing

Consider the colors of the rainbow: violet, indigo, blue, green, yellow, orange, and red. Use these seven colors to represent a name(s) or some way(s) in which God has shown you love in your life. Start within your own home and then expand outward to your place of work, your neighborhood, your world.

_____

_____

_____

_____

›› Action

Give a donation to a charity of your choice, making it clear with an enclosed note that this donation represents your attempt to thank God for all the ways in which God's love has been showered on you.

›› Closing Prayer

Sweet Jesus, you are the greatest sign of God's love. I pledge to be more aware each day of the signs of your loving presence. Give me new eyes and a heart open to receive you. Amen.

day 8

Gift of Water,
Gift of Life

›› Introduction

It's pretty hard to survive in life without water. Daily you are
reminded of its health benefits in ads extolling the need for ten
glasses a day, warnings not to get dehydrated in the sun or when
exercising, even the conservation of water so that there is enough
for everyone. The human body is over seventy-five percent water.
That alone should tell you how vital it is to your well-being. Is it an
accident that water is essential to your spiritual well-being, as well?

›› Scripture

A few...were saved through water. 1 Peter 3:20

And baptism...now saves you. 1 Peter 3:21

›› Reflection

Few remember when the well was the center of neighborhood life
or relate to the majority of the world where lives depend on the
absence or presence of water. You turn on a faucet and voilá!, water.
It has become just another thing you take for granted, like air. But

water is more awesome than its power to sustain your physical life. Through baptism, it provides you a water-way to eternal life. Baptism is the source of your spiritual link to God. It is your connection to others. Through baptism, you become one with the family of Christ. Through baptism, you share in Christ's mission. Through baptism, you enter the paschal mystery of suffering and death and rise to eternal life.

All of this is received through the waters of baptism. Through it, you join a royal priesthood of those marked with the sign of Christ. This is the salvation for which people yearn. It is the redemption they crave. Baptism, God's claim on the soul, forever.

>> GIFT OF LIFE

Water
> Thirst quencher
> Life-giver
> Splash of the everlasting

Water
> Common element
> More precious than gold
> Creative power
> Destructive force

Tears,
> Rivers,
> Stagnant pools,
> Raindrops, thunderstorms, gentle spring showers

Water
> Poured from a shell
> Mingled with holy words
> Words of salvation

Across the world,
> Beyond divisions of race, creed, and lineage
> Eternal bonds of grace.

›› Ways to Honor the Gift of Water

Water is symbolic of life, so how you regard and use water is representative of how you treat the gift of life itself. Use these rituals to give increased awareness and honor to water as the "holy" water of God's blessing and call.

- Place a bowl of clear water in your entry hall. Each time you enter or leave, bless yourself.
- Fill a bowl, or vase, or clear glass with water. Hold it up to the sunshine and watch it twinkle. Give thanks.
- Pour water over your hands, arms, or feet, and with each pouring, pray that this part of your body will always be used for God's greater glory.

›› Reflection/Journal Writing

Baptism is the water of eternal life. It is a bath for the soul, membership in the family of God. What do you remember of your baptism? If you were an adult when you were baptized you probably remember a great deal. Write the details in your journal: the time and place, the names of your godparents and why you chose them, the priest who baptized you and those who were present to celebrate this moment. What did you wear? Were there any special festivities? What is the significance of your baptismal name?

If you were baptized as a baby, search out your baptismal record. Answer the same questions by doing a little research and talking with those who were present. Write about what significance your baptism has for you now that it may not have had before.

›› Action

Find your baptismal certificate or send for a copy if yours is lost. Frame it and place it in your prayer space with a small votive candle that you can light whenever you come to pray. Allow it to remind you of the gift you've been given and what it costs to live it out with integrity.

›› Closing Prayer

Place water in a small bowl, or use the bowl in your entry hall. Dip your fingers in the water as you make the sign of the cross, and say this prayer:

I recommit myself to the service of the Lord, in the name of the Father, and of the Son, and of the Holy Spirit. Amen.

Temptation Overcome by Faith

›› INTRODUCTION

You are coming to the end of your first full week of living on purpose. It seems fitting that you look at temptation, for you probably experienced it many times this week as you attempted to stay true to the covenant you signed on the first day. But what does it mean to be tempted? Words like lured, enticed, coaxed, attracted, and pulled try to capture the nature of temptation. If you have known temptation (and who has not?), each of these words describes a particular aspect of its mysterious and deceptive energy.

Today's reflections lead you more deeply into the temptations of Christ in the wilderness, just prior to his public ministry. Pay special attention. You, too, can encounter lures that can lead you away from God's will for your life.

›› SCRIPTURE

He was in the wilderness forty days, tempted by Satan. MARK 1:13

›› REFLECTION

These weeks of committed renewal are an especially good time to reflect on Christ's temptations in the desert. Jesus models for you how to resist the enticements to sin and evil that you encounter in your daily life. He shows you how to make right choices so that you can truly be a beloved child of God. Jesus is alone with Satan and Satan is trying to learn who Jesus really is. In the midst of their dialogue, Jesus confirms his own self-understanding. While Mark doesn't go into detail, we know that Satan tried to lure Jesus away from his understanding of God's covenant revealed in the scriptures and from his understanding of the calling he received at his baptism.

Interestingly, Satan can be translated, "the hinderer." Jesus' temptations, like yours, are anything, anyone, any relationship, idea, event or reality that tries to keep you from living fully your call to be a follower of Christ and child of God. You learn who you really are when you are tempted and are forced to make choices. Hopefully, your choices affirm your relationship with God.

›› WITH JESUS IN THE WILDERNESS

Jesus
    Alone with the one who hinders
    Alone to ponder what
    God has written on his heart
Jesus
    Alone in a dangerous place
    Hungry for bread
    Chasing only purpose
Jesus
    Coaxed to tempt God's love
    To avoid suffering and death
    Desiring only integrity
Jesus
    Lured to the edge of the abyss
    Offered a world of power
    Seeking only to serve

Jesus
    Finding himself
    In the struggle to choose
    Banishing temptation
    With faithfulness to God's word

›› Legitimate Needs Lead to Temptation

After forty days and nights, Jesus was justifiably hungry. Satan used his hunger to tempt him to prove his power. When you neglect your legitimate needs, or confuse your wants and your needs, you can expect to struggle with temptation. Your needs present a variety of choices as to how you will satisfy them. Put yourself in Jesus' place. Imagine his hunger after his long fast. Reflect on what you are fasting from during these forty days of renewal: TV, idle gossip, food, spending money, unwise use of time, and so on. Has your fast led you to temptation? How did you choose to respond? Do Jesus' strength and words offer you encouragement?

›› Reflection/Journal Writing

Continue to reflect on Jesus' experience with the temptations of Satan. Reflect too on your own temptations. How many of them are linked to your real unmet needs? Who or what tries to hinder you from belonging to the Lord with your whole mind, heart, and soul? Write down some of those needs and identify some of these hindrances. What can you do to defeat these hindrances while still meeting your needs with authentic and legitimate choices?

›› Action

Choose one need in your own life that isn't being met and brainstorm alone or with a trusted friend or adviser how you can meet that need in a way that allows you to have integrity and follow God's word.

›› Closing Prayer

Jesus, my brother, you were tempted, as I am, to put aside God's word, to ignore the call written on your heart. Be with me and strengthen me to meet each new temptation with the choice to belong only to God. Amen.

Repent and Believe

›› INTRODUCTION

How does it feel to know that you have kept your agreement to live on purpose, to live with God as the priority in your life, for ten days now? On the second day, you took the step of trying to reconcile yourself to God by saying you are sorry for not keeping God as the top priority in your life. Today, you reflect more deeply on this theme of repentance, especially as you hear it proclaimed by Jesus in Mark's gospel. Open your heart, once again. Allow yourself to be in the crowd, listening to Jesus say, "Repent!"

›› SCRIPTURE

Repent and believe the good news. MARK 1:15

›› REFLECTION

The only thing that can give you the courage to confess your failings is believing the good news of God's unconditional love. It seems so simple: believe the good news so that you can repent. Repent so that you can experience the good news. Repentance is both an experience and a result of faith. Because you believe that God's love has no bounds and that nothing can separate you from God's love, you can have the courage and the humility to express your sorrow for the times you have abused or ignored that love. When you repent, you actually experience the very love you believe exists. This experience of God's love propels you to an even greater desire to love God, and to the realization of what you have missed and are now able to recover.

>> SOUL SISTERS

Repentance
    and faith;
    sisters in the soul.
Together they lead you
    to God's heart.
Together they tell you
    of God's love and forgiveness.
Repentance and faith
    emptying the heart of whatever
    clogs its embrace of God;
Filling the soul
    with feelings of awe,
        of gratitude,
        of joy.
Repent and believe:
    see God's face.

>> THE WAY OF REPENTANCE

It can be difficult to seek repentance because you often cannot see your own faults and weaknesses. Worse, you resist allowing others to point these things out. Yet every difficult task can be accomplished if you break it down into doable steps. Try these six steps when you need to repent.

• The first step: acknowledge sin—your own.
• The second step: express sorrow.
• The third step: throw yourself on God's mercy.
• The fourth step: resolve to change.

- The fifth step: change.
- The final step: express gratitude for God's help and love.

›› Reflection/Journal Writing

Repentance is an act of change, restoration, and grace. It is not enough to say the words, "I am sorry." They must be followed by behavioral change. If you speak or act unkindly toward others, then repentance would lead to words and acts of kindness. If you abuse your body or act in violent ways, then true repentance would find you taking care of yourself, leading a healthy life and finding peaceful ways to deal with conflict.

Write about some of the thoughts, attitudes, or behaviors for which you need to repent. Describe how these would change after your repentance.

_____

_____

_____

_____

_____

›› Action

Using Jesus' command to, "repent and believe the good news," write a prayer of repentance, asking God to show you the state of your heart and what you need to confess. Keep this prayer in your Bible and use it whenever you need to repent. Consider receiving the sacrament of reconciliation at some time during these forty days.

›› Closing Prayer

Loving God, forgive me my arrogance, my hard heart, my fear of being honest about my life. Give me the humility to turn myself inside out so that I can confront my sin and change my ways. I ask this in the spirit of Jesus, who said, "Repent." Amen.

God's Claim on Our Lives

›› INTRODUCTION

God and Abraham had already established a relationship of trust. Wasn't this the same God who called Abram and changed his name, who tested Abraham and Sarah by promising them a son when they had given up hope of ever conceiving one? Didn't this God lead Abraham out of the desert and promise that he would father a nation? God did all this and more because of Abraham's integrity and faithfulness. This time God asked the most improbable and excruciating test, the life of Abraham's beloved son. Would Abraham trust enough to pass the test?

Today you pray about the claim God has on your life and whether or not your trust is sufficient to follow God's will in all things—even those that seem most outlandish.

›› SCRIPTURE

"Abraham!" And he said, "Here I am." GENESIS 22:1

›› REFLECTION

God knows you by name. And that's not all. God knows who you are underneath the layers of defense you've learned to use as a cover. God knows your character, what you are capable of doing with your life. Your feelings, best intentions, flaws, and personal challenges are all known to God. Even the parts of your life that you don't know or understand do not escape God's knowledge.

When God looks at you, God sees who you were made to be. God sees the purpose of your life, given to you "before you were knit in your mother's womb." God gave Abraham a test that Abraham had the ability to pass, though to others it seemed impossible. Does knowing this give you hope?

>> OPEN TO GOD'S CALL

Abraham
>   Ancient nomad
>   Desert dweller
>   Seeker
You welcomed strangers
>   And entertained angels
You offered your best
>   Cakes
>   Drink
>   Self
Abraham
>   Faithful husband
>   Doting father
>   Son of God
You trusted God's will
>   In spite of a broken heart
>   In spite of not understanding
>   In spite of not seeing
>   The future
Abraham—mentor on the road of faith.

›› Deciding to Give Your Life

Like Abraham, the most challenging dilemmas that come your way involve people and things you love, those who fill up your heart and monopolize your thoughts and choices. You don't receive challenges to kill. You are not commanded to destroy. But you are asked to choose. Are you willing to sacrifice everything and everyone in order to follow God's will for your life? Who will determine your priorities in life, God or someone else? The primary choice of the spiritual life is whether or not the purpose of your life is driven by God's will or by someone else's.

• When you need to make an important decision, who do you turn to first for guidance?
• When life is challenging and you feel confused, who do you turn to first for advice?
• When you can't see the future and you're afraid to make hard choices that might cause you anguish, who do you turn to first for strength and clarity?

›› Reflection/Journal Writing

Are you struggling with choices right now? Is there something or someone you are being called to sacrifice so that the purpose of your life can be fulfilled? Take some time now to describe how you handle the choices that cross your life. Can you improve? Are you and God partners? Are you able to say, "Here I am," when God asks you to do that which is difficult in the pursuit of your life's purpose?

_____

_____

_____

_____

_____

_____

›› ACTION

Offer your sacrifice to God. Get a small ceramic bowl. On a strip of paper, write a few words that describe a sacrifice you must make to live on purpose. Place the paper in the bowl. Light and burn the paper as a symbol of your desire to make this sacrifice with trust that God will bring your sincere effort to good. As you watch the paper burn, pray the prayer below and feel free to add any other thoughts you may wish to express.

›› CLOSING PRAYER

O God of Abraham, show me the way. You ask me to offer you all that I am, everything I have, my whole heart and soul. I want to be totally yours. Accept this offering and give me in return, your strength and your love. It is enough. Amen.

The Lord Will Provide

>> INTRODUCTION

Providence—divine providence—seems like an old-fashioned word, a concept out of a church of long ago. Whatever happened to our dependence on God for all things? Why do we so seldom hear the words "divine providence" anymore? In days gone by, many people heard their elders say, "God will provide," when food was scarce or illness threatened, or the world seemed out of control. What do you say now? Who do you rely on? Lean back into God's providence today, and see where it leads you.

>> SCRIPTURE

So Abraham called that place "the Lord will provide." GENESIS 22:14

>> REFLECTION

Today, follow Abraham and Isaac as they make their way up the mountain to offer their sacrifice. Isaac doesn't seem to know he is part of the plan revealed to Abraham. He seems to go with his father willingly, naively, trusting that no harm will come to him. At one point, Isaac even carries the wood for the sacrifice. Eventually, he realizes that there is no sacrificial lamb. When he asks, his father assures him that God will provide the offering. Again, Isaac trusts his father just as Abraham trusts his father, God. Even as Isaac is tied to the altar as a living sacrifice of praise to God, the knife raised to kill him, we read no words of struggle, no pleading, no fighting against this unjust situation.

This story is so unlike anything that exists in most real life situations today. Would even the most trusting child go hiking with a parent and not complain about carrying the supplies? Would the most trusting child allow him or herself to be tied to an altar, knowing it is the place of sacrifice, without a cry of outrage, without tears and shouts for help? How can it be that both Abraham and Isaac trust the one they love so completely that they do not question what seems so wrong? Can it be that Abraham believed his son was a gift who belonged, in truth, to God? Could it be that Isaac knew somewhere deep inside that God could be trusted with his life? The ways of God are mysterious to all but those who trust completely.

›› OFFER YOURSELF

Isaac,
> Child of laughter
> Long-awaited
> Precious

You grew in wisdom,
> Age and grace

You honored and trusted
> Your parents
> Your heritage
> Your God

Isaac,
> Did your intuition
> Cause your foot to hesitate?
> What did you think when no lamb appeared
>> But you?

Did your lip quiver? Were you afraid
　　To offer yourself
　　　　Entirely?
Isaac,
　　Body and soul
　　Heart and mind
　　Every limb, every fiber, every moment
　　　　Of joy and sorrow
　　You gave them all.
You gave your all.

›› SELF-SACRIFICE

The twenty-first century doesn't offer many calls for self-sacrifice. It is an age where most only do what will bring rewards and shy away from anything that hints of sacrifice. After September 11, 2001, you heard many stories of brave men and women who offered themselves in the hope of saving others. Throughout time, you hear war stories of soldiers who risk their lives to save their comrades. Yet, except in extraordinary circumstances, who lays down a life so that others can live?

Abraham's willingness to sacrifice his son calls you to examine the role self-sacrifice plays in your own life. To sacrifice your "self" is to let go of the need to be the center of the universe, to have the world revolve around your wishes, needs, and demands. To sacrifice your self is to let your ego die, to believe that there is One who knows better than you what you need in life. To sacrifice your self is to accept that there is a God, and it is not you.

Reflect on the past week and note the times when you could have sacrificed your self but didn't; any time when you tried to play God with your own or another's life; any time when you showed by word or action that your self was more important than finding and following God's purpose for your life.

›› Reflection/Journal Writing

It isn't easy to die to self. Actually, it's hard work to put your ego in its place: at the feet of God's will. It takes a special self-awareness and honesty to cultivate true humility. Do you have it? Do you believe that God will help you get it? Write awhile in your journal about the place of humility and sacrifice in your life. Ask God for what you need; it's the first step in dying to self.

_____

_____

_____

_____

_____

_____

›› Action

Find a local mission, soup kitchen, or thrift store. Volunteer to do the grubbiest, lowest job they have, one no one else wants to do. As you go about your work, do so with a smile and a pleasant attitude, thinking about the self-sacrifice that is pleasing to God.

›› Closing Prayer

God of Abraham and Isaac, show me the way to humble acceptance of your will for my life. Soften my heart and bend my ego so that I may become more able to sacrifice my self for love of you. Amen.

We Cannot Be Separated from God

>> INTRODUCTION

When you read Paul's letter to the Romans, remember you are reading a teaching about God's love. Paul uses every image at his disposal to describe the kind of redeeming love God has for you; to describe a God who not only loves, but *is* love. This letter urges the Romans to embrace this God of love with their entire being. It's also a practical look at how turning over your mind, heart, and spirit is the basic requirement for living a life in Christ. In your reflection today, keep in mind that this letter is addressed to you, "all God's beloved…who are called to be saints" (Romans 1:7).

>> SCRIPTURE

Who will separate us from the love of Christ? ROMANS 8:35

>> REFLECTION

You have heard that God is love. It's ingrained on your psyche. Yet you may doubt that this God of love can truly love you. You may doubt that you are worthy of a God so lavish in unconditional love. You may resist God's advances because you don't believe what you have been told: "nothing can separate us from the love of God in Christ Jesus…" (Romans 8:39). It is a vicious cycle of yearning and resignation; of seeking and refusal to accept.

Earlier this week Abraham's faith in God's goodness and mercy was tested. He believed himself worthy of God's love, and God's love was poured out on him. Yesterday, you leaned on God's providence, God's care for your well-being, and your need to sacrifice your self in order to give yourself fully to God's providence. Both concepts are difficult, yet not so hard as today's invitation to set aside your self-importance and believe that the God of love, who loved you into existence, loves you each moment of each day, with all your failings and glory. Only you can separate yourself from God's love.

›› GOD'S LOVE

Like a tree
    Roots deeply entrenched in the earth
    Inseparable from the soil that feeds its existence
    So is God's love
Like moss
    That anchors itself to tree bark
    And weaves its way into every fiber
    So is God's love
Like shells
    Embedding themselves on rocks
    Cemented in place forever
    So is God's love
Nothing can wedge itself
    Between God's love and the beloved
Nothing can dissolve that
    Bond
God is love
    And you, created and fashioned by Love,
        Are the beloved.

›› The Quality of God's Love

Love is an elusive word. It is used to describe everything from teenage emotion to sacrificial offering of self for another. Love has been used throughout history to justify selfishness, to set nations against each other, and to support killing. Love has been used as a weapon when, in truth, true love is defenseless. St. Paul tells about love and you would do well today to remember these qualities that define both God's love, and what you strive to offer God and others.

Love is patient, kind,
>   not envious or arrogant or rude,
>   not insistent on its own way,
>   not irritable or resentful,
>   does not rejoice in wrongdoing, rejoices in the truth,
>   bears all things, believes all things, hopes, endures,
>   never ends (1 Corinthians 13:4–8).

›› Reflection/Journal Writing

As you reflect on the quality of God's love and God's inability to be separate from those loved, recall any times in your life when you felt separated from God. Perhaps you were angry, doubtful, or confused. Maybe you were not able to feel a personal connection and your faith was not strong enough to carry you through your time of alienation or pride. Write about those times. What happened to bring you back? What or who helped you to recognize God's presence, unshakable and real?

>> ACTION

Make a list of each of the qualities of love mentioned previously. Put one quality on each line and then next to it, write some definite person, place, or situation in your life that will benefit from your demonstration of this quality of love during the rest of the year.

>> CLOSING PRAYER

God of love and mercy, I believe that nothing I can say, do, think, or feel can separate me from your love. Help my unbelief. Amen.

Listening: Passport to Spiritual Growth

›› INTRODUCTION

Listening is a key theme throughout Scripture. The ability to listen is both a skill and an art; you can't live on purpose without the desire and the effort to listen. Most people believe they know how to listen because they can hear, but they couldn't be more wrong. Hearing and listening are two different things. The first is a matter of physical health, the latter, a conscious effort to honor and understand. Today, you reflect on how well you listen, especially how well you listen to God, who became flesh in Jesus Christ.

›› SCRIPTURE

"This is my Son, the beloved, listen to him!" MARK 9:7

›› REFLECTION

At the top of the mountain, Peter, James, and John heard God's voice commanding them to listen to Jesus. Scripture says, "They were terrified." Can you imagine it? Do you think they were terrified by the event, or by the realization of what it would cost them to listen to Jesus?

Jesus is the one who shows us who God is, revealing God's nature through his words and actions. If you are sincere about living your life on purpose, then listen, on purpose, to what Jesus has to say to your life. Do you wonder what God wants of you? Listen to Jesus teach about discipleship. Are you curious about how to build the right kind of relationships? Listen to Jesus as he interacts with others, with love. Are you searching for how to endure the sufferings of your life? Listen to Jesus as he accepts the cross and embraces his own suffering. Have no doubt. If you listen to Jesus, there will be a cost: your life.

›› LISTEN!

Speak, Lord, your servant is listening!
Remove the wax from my ears,
>   breathe into them
>   clear a passageway that
>   funnels your will into my spirit.
Soften any hardness in my heart;
>   melt the resentments.
Create a new heart in me,
>   one that cherishes your word above all else.
Blow the fog from my eyes;
>   wipe away the blindness.
Give me eyes that
>   see the needs of the beloved ones.
Speak to me of hope,
>   faith,
>   love.
Your servant is listening.

›› Learn to Listen

Listening is a skill, and as such, there are practical steps you can take to improve how you listen. These apply to your efforts to listen to God as well as to others. Let's look at some things you can do to improve your listening skills.

- Face the speaker directly.
- Make eye contact.
- Watch what the body says to be sure you understand how it affects the meaning of the conversation.
- Be quiet. If you are doing all the talking, you won't have time to listen.
- Ask questions for clarification if you aren't sure what something means.
- Summarize what you hear, briefly, rather than just assume you understand.
- Keep your heart open, able to be influenced.

›› Reflection/Journal Writing

When was the last time God spoke to you? What did you hear? Did God's message come through someone else's voice? Did it come through an experience? Did you hear God through something or someone you saw? What is the message God has given you, in and through Christ? Write about your experience of listening to God and how Christ facilitates God's message to you. Ask for whatever you need to improve your ability to listen to Christ.

_____

_____

_____

_____

_____

_____

>> Action

Choose a word, phrase, passage, or story from Scripture in which Jesus speaks to you, personally. Write it on a plain piece of paper and post the paper where you will see it daily.

>> Closing Prayer

Jesus, beloved of God, speak, for I am listening. Amen.

Only Jesus

›› INTRODUCTION

If you haven't figured it out yet, there is only one person who can be depended on one hundred percent of the time to give you what you need. That is Jesus Christ. Today you have the perfect opportunity to recognize this spiritual reality and to rededicate yourself to this relationship. It is the only personal relationship that will give your life purpose. It is the only personal relationship that will not disappoint, that produces what it promises.

Jesus Christ is the only one who can transform your life. Sure, it will take your cooperation; but, even with all the personal effort in the world, you won't be able to live on purpose if your eyes are not on Jesus.

›› SCRIPTURE

Suddenly when they looked around, they saw no one with them any more, but only Jesus. MARK 9:8

›› REFLECTION

Peter, James, and John spent a lot of time with Jesus. They knew he sought solitude for prayer, especially after being with crowds. They expected that this hike up the mountain would be ordinary, like their other prayer-escapes. What a surprise!

The disciples took prayer, Jesus, and God's power for granted, minimizing God's ability to break into life with power and glory. They expected too little of God, of Jesus, and of themselves. They thought they knew Jesus, but they had no idea who he was or what he wanted to teach them. Now they return to their "ordinary" lives with the realization that every creature is extraordinary, filled with God's glory. Their prayer has taught them that it is Jesus, and Jesus alone, who makes each person, each day, each encounter, glorious.

›› Only Jesus

Suddenly,
>You realize you are not God
>>You cannot
>>Control the universe
>You cannot
>>Control your own
>>Small world
Too often, you live as though
>All depends
>>On you
>Life and death, depends
>>On you
>Success or failure, depends
>>On you
Suddenly,
>You see that there is
>>Only Jesus
>You realize that none can satisfy,
>>Only Jesus
You surrender
>To the glory that is Jesus
You turn over your heart, your being
>your control,
>>Only to Jesus.

›› Stay Focused On Jesus

Staying focused on Jesus, and being content with only Jesus is not easy in a world that daily bombards you with what you "need" in order to be happy. Your heart may desire Jesus and your mind may believe Jesus is whom you seek…but somehow, your will wants control and you are torn between your inner truth and the messages of the world around you. To tune out these false idols and embrace Jesus in your daily life is difficult, but not impossible. Try these tips:

- Each morning, when you wake, make a morning offering.
- Listen to Christian music and fill your spirit with Jesus' company.
- Throughout the day, whenever you see yourself clinging to control, pray, "Only Jesus."
- At night, before you sleep, turn your cares, troubles, and worries over to Jesus.

›› Reflection/Journal Writing

It's time now to have a personal talk with Jesus. Imagine yourself leaving a prayer experience where your heart was filled with God's majesty and Jesus' glory. You are walking down from the mountaintop. The path winds and twists before you. Suddenly, you hear the quiet. In the place of trees and vegetation, you see Jesus. The nature around you sighs of Jesus. Write your thoughts and feelings as you see your Lord and Savior walking by your side during this second week of renewal. Confide in him what you need to strengthen you for the weeks ahead.

_____

_____

_____

_____

_____

_____

>> Action

Make a special effort this week to participate in the Eucharist, where the Body of Christ transforms the cross into glory. Receive the Eucharist and spend some special time alone with Jesus.

>> Closing Prayer

Lord Jesus, I offer you my day, my life, my whole being. I accept your rule over my life and I turn my eyes to you today, only you. Keep me focused on your glory, Lord, so that I can deal with the crosses that life sends. Amen.

Stir Up Your Gratitude and Praise

>> INTRODUCTION

Are you tired of trying to live on purpose? Are you discouraged because you may have had some failures in your commitment? Well hold on, because today's gospel, the Transfiguration, will stir up hope, encourage your perseverance, and motivate you to look toward new life so that you don't get mired in the suffering of the cross. We can only hope that the glory the apostles experienced on that mountaintop led them to prayers of gratitude and visions of their own glory. That's what you want to concentrate on today: not your failures, but the experience of God's glory and love that is embedded in your own being. Take time today to give thanks for what God is doing in your life, through Jesus Christ.

>> SCRIPTURE

Then Peter said, "It is good for us to be here." MARK 9:5

›› REFLECTION

When good things happen, aren't you glad? Don't you want to raise the roof with words of gratitude and joy? When good things happen, especially when you don't expect them or have done nothing to deserve them, you are humbled. You write thank-you notes, make phone calls, send flowers, or e-mail cards. In other words, you recognize your good fortune and don't hold back your gratitude.

That's what Peter was expressing when, awed by the sights and sounds around him, he tells Jesus "it is good for us to be here." It was good because it showed Peter that if he held fast to Jesus, everything would make sense. It was good because it convinced Peter that Jesus was the one they had been awaiting, the Messiah. It was good because Peter learned that he was not only special to Jesus; but also, that he was being given a glimpse of "the living God" in whose image all are created.

Peter's gratitude erupted in a desire to keep the experience alive, not to let it go. Little did he realize that the one way to keep the experience of God's living presence, in Jesus, alive, is to welcome and embrace that presence within your own life, the lives of others, and of all creation.

›› GIVE THANKS

Praise the Lord
> My spirit

Sing God's praise

Praise God
> For the days of hardship
> For the times of despair

Praise God
> For the brilliance of humanity
>> Formed from God's love

Give thanks
> Every breath of my being

Every bone and muscle
Each and every cell
Give thanks
For God is worthy
God is great
And I,
I am God's image
Give thanks.

›› GLORY LIST

Today, after two weeks of reflection, prayer, and action in your effort to live on purpose, take some time to make a list of all the ways in which you reflect God's glory. What are your best characteristics, your gifts and strengths, your genuine qualities of caring? What are things for which you want to be remembered? What has God revealed to you about your own spiritual glory, in these two weeks?

›› REFLECTION/JOURNAL WRITING

Write a thank-you note to God for all that is your life. Write it as a psalm, or poem, a letter, or any way that expresses for you the deepest mystery of your gratitude and praise for who God is and how God's presence is being realized in your life.

_____

_____

_____

_____

_____

_____

›› ACTION

The most sincere form of gratitude is not offered in words, but in action. Your glory as a child of God and heir, with Jesus, of heaven, is shared by all of creation. All creation reflects God's glory.

Go out and collect some leaves or flowers or rocks or any samples of nature and bring them to your prayer space. What does your collection tell you about who God is? who you are?

›› Closing Prayer

I thank you, my God, for I am so awesomely made. You have filled all of creation with your glory. Saturate me with respect for you and all that you have created. Amen.

Getting Rid of Idols

›› INTRODUCTION

The very first instruction God gave Moses was to honor God alone, to make no idols. All the other commandments eventually come back to this one. It is reinforced in Jesus' teaching that you should love God with all your heart, soul, mind, and will, and your neighbor as yourself. So the greatest commandment, heard from the burning bush and from Jesus, is to love God above all. Everything flows from this love and without it, all other love is impossible.

Today you reflect on whether you have followed that command to banish idols and love God. You'll examine the idols in your life and what it will take to step away from them and return God to the center of your purpose, worship, and devotion.

›› SCRIPTURE

You shall not have false gods before me. EXODUS 20:3

›› REFLECTION

The use of the term "idol" might be misleading here. You might be tempted to think that because you don't have statues or trinkets depicting other religions that you don't have idols. Wrong! Idols are anything or anyone that has the power to determine your choices in life; to claim your devotion. They are anything or anyone that replaces Christ as the source of your inspiration and happiness, anything or anyone that diverts your life's purpose from pleasing and honoring God, above all.

Are any of these idols in your life: money, prestige, power, influence over others, the accumulation of things, popularity, having your own way, thinking you are better than others? If so, don't rush over this issue of idol-making. The first step in getting rid of idols is seeing reality.

>> God's Name Is Love

Did you ever build
    a golden calf
    hoping it would
        save you from yourself?
Do you stockpile
    treasures while the
    world goes hungry?
False gods are everywhere.
But you, you have the power to
    cast out your idols,
    to cling to the one God
        visible in Jesus Christ.
And God's name is love,
    God's nature is giving,
    God's response is mercy,
    God's joy is repentance.
There are no other gods before or to come.
God's name is love.

>> Getting Rid of Idols

If only you could take a stick and smash all your idols and be done with them. Unfortunately, it doesn't work that way. Idols, false gods, are insidious creatures. They weave their way into the fabric of your life. Sometimes they look like a good thing, like trying to earn more money and live in a bigger house in a better neighborhood. Sometimes they have become part of your patterned response, like being a "control freak." Much of what masquerades as an idol isn't bad, in itself. It becomes an obstacle to spiritual growth when it begins to consume you, when it violates the spirit of the gospel, when it is no longer a source of love for self, God, and others.

One way to rid yourself of idols is to examine your conscience. Each night before sleep, relax in the quiet and think about your day. Did you make choices that were selfish or lacked respect for others? Did your desire to acquire things, control, or "shine" cause you to speak or act without love? When you had the chance, did you try to live as though you were the only Bible some people will ever read? Based on what you see in your reflection, you will begin to recognize the false gods that dominate your life.

›› Reflection/Journal Writing

In the twenty-first century, both the state and religion have become the focus of devotion, over the commands of God. Rather than love, humanity seems susceptible to building every kind of idol that cannot satisfy. What about you? Write today about your own experience of idolatry. Are there people, things, attitudes, or behaviors in your life that demonstrate your resistance to love? What is worth your dedication? Who is worth your devotion?

_____

_____

_____

_____

_____

_____

>> ACTION

Write the names of your idols on separate small pieces of paper. Collect them in a small box or biodegradable bag and bury them in your yard as you pray the prayer that follows.

>> CLOSING PRAYER

There is one God, visible in Jesus Christ. I will not allow false gods to take up residence in my heart. Amen.

Can Anger Ever Be a Virtue?

›› INTRODUCTION

Jesus was a human being, exactly as you are, except for sin. So when you see Jesus become angry and aggressive with the money changers in the temple, you have to believe that anger, in itself, is not sinful or else Jesus could not have been angry. Could it be that God's anger has qualities that differ from yours and from which you can learn? How do you know when your anger is like God's and when it is sinful?

›› SCRIPTURE

Making a whip of cords, he drove them all out of the temple.... JOHN 2:15

›› REFLECTION

Anger is a normal human feeling, neither good nor bad. What you do with your anger, however, can change your life and those of others. Why do the words of some fuel your anger, but others can say the same and it does not affect you? How can you overlook the abusive or unjust activities of some and rail against others?

Two Greek words used in the New Testament for our English word "anger" are *orge,* meaning "passion, energy;" and *thumos,* meaning "agitated, boiling." Biblically, anger is God-given energy intended to help you solve problems. God's anger is in response to injustice and consistently directed toward the ways in which humans hurt each other, especially the most vulnerable. It is full of truth. It sees through sham, pretense, and hypocrisy to the core of brokenness. Ironically, God gifted you with anger so that you could care for creation as a just steward, assuring the right use of resources, preserving human dignity, and fostering peace.

In today's reading, Jesus' "zeal" for God was stirred to the boiling point and exposed the duplicity of a temple where God, who was to come first, is overshadowed by the greed of the marketplace.

›› Destroy This Temple

Jesus seems
>Undone

He bursts into the temple
>And scatters the
>Idol-makers

He uses force
>To set things right

He is righteous in the pursuit
>Of God's work
>>Not self-righteous
>>But full of his true self
>Full of grace

His anger restores
>The temple to
>What it was meant to be
>Filled with God
>Holy

A place where God reigns.

›› Making Anger Holy

Who hasn't been angry? Who hasn't acted in anger, only to regret the outcome? Here are a few tips on making your anger "of God" and not sinful.

- Acknowledge when your anger is selfish and your angry behavior is sinful.
- Ask forgiveness of those your anger has offended.
- Recognize God's presence even in the most difficult or hurtful of persons and situations.
- Trust God to take care of every situation; don't play God.
- Act out of the good in your own heart not in retaliation for what has been done to you.
- Attack the problem, not the person, through good communication.
- Speak the truth in love.
- Practice replacing your angry habits or words with words of love and acts of goodness.

›› Reflection/Journal Writing

As you reflect on the role of anger in your life, try to evaluate it honestly. How often are you angry at others because of feelings you don't know how to express? How often is your anger hurtful to others, or yourself? Is your anger ever directed against injustice, or are your motives less noble? Write about anger in your life and what you might do to become part of the way of peace rather than remain part of the problem of violence.

_____

_____

_____

_____

_____

_____

›› ACTION

Research Catholic/Christian justice organizations that work to right injustices and/or to empower the poor to better lives. Join one of these organizations and contribute your resources and talent to furthering their work. You can begin by going to your Internet search engine and entering the words: Catholic justice organizations.

›› CLOSING PRAYER

O God, your anger rages against those who choose to live life at the expense of the lowly. Transform my heart. Help me to cleanse the temple of my life of anything unjust. Use my anger to change the world. Amen.

Fool for Christ

>> INTRODUCTION

Have you ever thought of God as foolish? Does it seem blasphemous to consider it? How about the cross of Christ? Does it seem a waste; the needless suffering of an innocent man? As you reflect on the cross today, prepare to think about how well you deal with paradox, i.e., a contradiction in terms. Can weakness be strength? Can foolishness be wisdom? Are you comfortable with mystery?

>> SCRIPTURE

For God's foolishness is wiser than human wisdom, and God's weakness is stronger than human strength. 1 CORINTHIANS 1:25

>> REFLECTION

For Paul, the cross is good news. Where others see defeat and shame, Paul sees the power and the glory of God. Again and again, Paul turns to the central paradox of the Christian life: salvation through the cross of Christ; new life through suffering and death accepted in faith and love.

God will never be known through rational knowledge, science, or reason. God did not create because it was the advisable thing to do; because it made good sense. God created in order to be in relationship, to radiate love, to rejoice in sharing the beauty of God's self. Was this wise or foolish? In the light of the violence, hatred, and atrocities committed throughout history, one might be tempted to say foolish. Yet, thinking of humanity's acts of selfless courage, sacrifice, and generosity, you could say wise.

To know God, you have to put aside the need to see signs in the heavens that prove God exists. Throw away the need to solve each question about God, to unravel each unexplainable mystery of the universe, life, and death. To know God, you must embrace God's ultimate wisdom, Jesus. To know God is to accept that the cross is the royal road to freedom; saving grace. Who is foolish, who is wise? God's wisdom is about faith.

>> Foolish Faith

At the foot of the cross
 it all becomes clear.
In the cross is our purpose,
 not despair
 but peace,
  serenity.
To those without faith,
 foolishness.
For those who believe,
 life
 love in action;
  undeniable.
Wisdom.

>> Who Is Wise?

In an age that marks the cross as a crutch for losers, you must hold it high despite your doubts and weakness. Draw a cross on a sheet of paper. On the vertical section of the cross, list the ways in which you feel spiritually weak, exhausted, or unable to bear the cross proudly. On the horizontal arms of the cross, put the names of those who are heroes in faith for you because they proclaim Christ boldly with their lives and give you strength.

›› Reflection/Journal Writing

Do you wear a cross? How do you feel about wearing a "sign of contradiction?" Can you be Christ's fool, preaching, with your life, the uncompromising way of the gospel? Or is that too hard in a world that demands prudent accommodation? Write with your heart, not your head.

_____

_____

_____

_____

_____

_____

›› Action

Choose a church and pray the Stations of the Cross. At each station, meditate on what the world might consider foolish about that event in Christ's walk of salvation and answer it with what you see as God's wisdom. For example, the world might see Veronica stepping out of the crowd in order to comfort Jesus as an unacceptable risk; after all, identifying herself as one who sympathized with Jesus, was not a popular thing to do in a hostile crowd. But God's wisdom sees a compassionate woman of faith who was willing to risk the consequences of acting in love.

›› Closing Prayer

Jesus, I fear the call to be your fool; I long for the grace to imitate your wisdom. Amen.

A Worthy Temple

›› INTRODUCTION

The Catholic Church teaches that the body is a temple of the Holy Spirit. It has used this image to impress upon youth the need to refrain from premarital sex, and above all, the need to only take healthy elements into the body, to respect the body in ways proper to one's state in life. It was an image that worked for many years. Do you think it still works today?

In a promiscuous society, the body is a personal possession that is worshiped but not respected. People believe they have the right to do whatever they wish with their own possessions. What about your temple? Is it a holy place or have you allowed it to become a "marketplace" for unhealthy attitudes, behaviors, and choices?

›› SCRIPTURE

Destroy this temple and in three days I will raise it up. JOHN 2:19

He was speaking of the temple of his body. JOHN 2:21

›› REFLECTION

There are two major body-related issues evident in this country. One is the booming cosmetics industry, where Americans spend millions of dollars annually to erase wrinkles, lose weight, change body features, and pamper themselves from head to toe. Is it because they want to please God by looking their best? Probably not. Another is the increased number of food related illnesses like anorexia, bulimia, and obesity crippling so many lives. People are literally starving or overfeeding themselves to death. Usually, both of these phenomena happen because men and women are not happy with their bodies. They want to look younger and avoid showing signs of age. They want to control lives that seem out of control. They self-medicate with food in order to stifle feelings of loneliness, rejection, and low self-esteem. It is epidemic.

Jesus talked about the temple of his body, the same temple you have, filled with the Spirit of God. Your temple was created to give God glory. Your temple is unique. Your temple has been entrusted to you as a gift to be cared for and honored. How are you doing so far?

›› You Cannot Destroy This Temple

It doesn't matter if
    the latest magazines
    are filled with pictures of young, thin models.
It doesn't matter if
    TV ads boom with music
    meant for agile, energetic youth.
Those are temples built
    on sand,
    confidence
        on what cannot last.
Your temple is the
    dwelling place of God,
        sacred flesh and blood.
Your temple doesn't need
    paint and perfume
    nips and tucks.

Your temple encases
  a pure heart
  a compassionate soul
  a passion for God's ways.
God gave you a worthy temple:
    living on purpose
        keeps it holy.

›› THE TEMPLE AT PRAYER

As a temple of the Holy Spirit, your body is a conduit for your prayer. Your body is one with your prayer, your conversation with God. Your posture can reflect outwardly what you feel inwardly: adoration, fear, distance, intimacy, reverence, joy, and so forth. So, as you pray, you are called to participate not only with your mind, heart, and soul but also with your body. Try some of these to increase your ability to make your temple a place of prayer:

- When at prayer, sit or stand in an upright position.
- Keep your feet flat on the floor, legs uncrossed.
- Allow your shoulders, arms, and ankles to relax.
- Place your hands, palms open, at rest in your lap, or one open palm cradling the other.
- When in meditative or contemplative mode, be comfortable enough to remain in the same position for at least ten minutes or longer.
- Always begin your time of prayer with deep inhaling and exhaling exercises to center your thoughts and relax your body.
- Don't forget to dance and make a joyful noise to the Lord whenever the Spirit moves you.

›› REFLECTION/JOURNAL WRITING

Use your journal time to have a heart-to-heart talk with Jesus about your body. Talk honestly about whether you like your body, whether or not you are respectful of its needs, how well you demand that others treat you with respect. There may be a few painful moments as you try to honestly speak the truth of your heart and soul. When you come to the end of your thoughts and feelings, ask Jesus to show you the beauty of your body and what it has allowed you to do for others during your lifetime. Write about that and your gratitude.

_____

_____

_____

_____

_____

›› ACTION

Bless your body today. Put a small amount of olive oil into a bowl and put a drop or two of perfume into it. Dip your finger into the oil and make the sign of the cross on your forehead, lips, eyes, ears, heart, arms, legs, and groin. At each blessing, ask the Lord to bless the beauty that is your body and to give you the grace to honor and respect it each and every day.

›› CLOSING PRAYER

Holy Spirit, shine from this temple of my body. Help me to accept, honor, and love my body and to expect others to do the same. Amen.

Becoming Real

›› INTRODUCTION

It has been said that people never truly know themselves, and without self-knowledge one cannot know another. Yet God knows you thoroughly and created who you are. Instead of sincerely seeking to know and understand yourself so that you can live faithful to who you were created to be, you may find that you often live falsely, forming yourself into who you think others want you to be. So today you will reflect on what it means to live authentically, with integrity. You will have the chance to renew your commitment to live on purpose, without falsehood.

›› SCRIPTURE

But Jesus…knew all people and needed no one to testify about anyone; for he himself knew what was in everyone. JOHN 2:24–25

›› REFLECTION

Today you have a great opportunity to examine the superficial character of many relationships. Why are so many people afraid to go deeper, love more intensely, get more personally involved, reveal their character and values, and stand for what is right and just? Perhaps it's because relationships are risky; they require a leap into the unknown. They don't guarantee long-term happiness, and few of us like to take risks.

Maybe that's why many fail to grow in relationship with Christ. Christ asks for risk. He invites a gift of your authentic self. He doesn't want the polite, politically correct, "nice at any cost," self-protective person you may offer in other relationships. Christ wants the person God made you to be, the real you, with all your flaws and all your glory. It's the only way that an authentic relationship can happen. People who avoid risk won't follow Christ, even if they are baptized Christians. People who are afraid to be authentically Christian wear the label, but never live out the call to discipleship.

Will you risk your whole life on the word of this man, Jesus? Is it too much to demand? The gospel passage today tells you that Jesus knows what is in everyone. He knows that you are capable of great things in God's name. He knows that you are afraid to "risk it all" on his behalf. He knows that you are tempted to deny him. He knows that idols find their way into your life. And he also knows that you are able to overcome everything, with his help, if you choose to do so.

›› Take a Risk
Jesus looked
    And his heart
    Was torn
People everywhere
    Clamored for his
    Attention
        His blessing
Everywhere
    People wore their
    Religion
        Like a badge of honor

While they lied
    Cheated and
        Ignored the poor at their door
Jesus took one look
    At each heart
    He saw the possibilities
    And the struggle
        He searched for those
        Who would risk it all
Whose badge would be
    The cross
    For love of him.

›› Becoming More Authentic

Most people, if given a choice, would say they want to live a more authentic and less "phony" life. But they seldom do so because they aren't sure what that means or how to achieve it. These general guidelines for greater authenticity imply risk. Are you ready?

- Let your "yes" mean "yes," and your "no" mean "no."
- Do not promise what you are unwilling or unable to fulfill.
- Speak up for what you believe rather than sit in silence when your values are under attack.
- Let your actions coincide with your words; "walk the talk."
- Participate in causes that support what you believe; be a visible not invisible participant in life.
- Expand your personal, social, and professional boundaries to include a wider and wider circle of ethnic, racial, religious, and cultural experiences and people.

›› Reflection/Journal Writing

Have you ever taken a risk in life? What gave you the courage to do so? Do you regret it or are you glad? If you believed that Jesus "knew what was in everyone," and you didn't need to hide behind a false self, would it give you strength to follow Jesus more boldly?

Make your writing today a dialogue with Jesus. Ask him to tell you about your real self, your authentic self. Ask him to assist you to risk what "seems" important for what really "is" important.

_____

_____

_____

_____

_____

_____

›› ACTION

Choose one person with whom you relate regularly and promise yourself to always speak the truth with this person, starting today. Don't allow yourself to rationalize or avoid; speak the truth in love.

›› CLOSING PRAYER

Jesus, my brother, you risked everything to be true to the person God sent to this earth. You spoke the truth in love, accepted the consequences, and changed the world. Grant me the courage to risk falsehood so that I can grow into my authentic self. Amen.

Keep Holy the Sabbath

›› INTRODUCTION

For many religions of the world, Saturday is the holiest day of the week, the Sabbath. Unlike Christians who promote Sunday as their holy weekday, other religions, like Judaism and Islam, cease work and give God praise and honor on Saturday. God thought Sabbath-keeping so important that it was made a commandment, in remembrance of God's own Sabbath-rest after the act of creation. As you reflect today on how well you honor the concept and the reality of Sabbath in your own life, do more than reflect: decide to make it a mainstay of your future.

›› SCRIPTURE

Remember the Sabbath and keep it holy. EXODUS 20:8

Six days you shall labor…but the seventh day is a Sabbath to the Lord your God; you shall not do any work…. EXODUS 20:9–10

The Lord blessed the Sabbath day and consecrated it. EXODUS 20:11

>> REFLECTION

Everyone craves rest, a slower pace, physical, mental, and spiritual renewal. But do you take the necessary time and creativity to actually meet these needs? Probably less often than is wise or holy.

Scripture declares that God was "pooped" after creating the heavens, the earth, and all that was in them. God's wisdom said to put aside all that "doing" and just "be" for a while. No matter the social value of the work, rest is an equal partner. Sabbath can be a day to play together or talk or take a nap. It takes the form of vacations, long weekends, camping trips, retreats. It's a time to let the inner person lie quiet so that God can break in.

Sabbath is a time to renew right relationships, to make people more important than money or influence, to shower God with attention and love. Sabbath can be thirty minutes each day praying and reflecting on the good news of God's love, a holy hour before the Blessed Sacrament, or a holy five minutes listening to rain on the roof. Sabbath is a disciplined cessation of purposeful activity as well as a state of mind, heart, and soul. It's about knowing who God is and giving honor with undivided attention.

>> SABBATH-KEEPING

Stop
　　Why can't I stop
　　　　All this frantic activity?
Why must I work too long hours
　　Too many days?
Why do I fail myself
　　My family
　　　　My God
　　By putting work and busyness
　　　　First
　　By believing all
　　　　Depends on me?

How do I begin to change?
    What should I do?
        What if I can't say "no?"
I long for time
    For quiet walks and talks
        With those I love
    For laughter and fun.
I long for rest
    Of body, mind, and spirit
        To let God be God.
I long for God
    To fill my life
        With meaning and love.
I long to live on purpose.

›› Ways to Keep the Sabbath Holy

Keeping the Sabbath is not another excuse to do lots of things. Rather, it is an opportunity to center yourself on God and renew your strength to live with purpose. As such, Sabbath-keeping can be practiced throughout the week, in many different ways. Here are some suggestions about how to begin.

- Take a two-minute break each hour to bless and thank God for one specific blessing.
- Call a local retreat center and book yourself into a retreat.
- Join a prayer group that meets weekly or monthly.
- Bring a spiritual book wherever you go and read it when stopped in traffic, waiting for an appointment, standing in a long line, or whenever the Spirit moves you. Or do the same with a rosary.
- Consecrate one day each week for your family to come together without an agenda or task, in order to spend time together. Begin this time with a prayer or ritual. If one day is impossible, then one evening or a few hours.
- Designate one evening each week for the family to eat together, no matter what. No problems will be solved at this meal, only

talking about what good is happening in each person's life. Take turns saying grace before and after the meal.

›› Reflection/Journal Writing

How Sabbath-oriented are you? Is carving out time to live a balanced life difficult for you? As you go through your day is it easy for you to incorporate time for God, or do you find it "just another chore?" As you write, pause every few minutes to simply be.

_____

_____

_____

_____

_____

_____

›› Action

Choose at least one of the Sabbath possibilities listed on the previous page. Commit to carrying it out. As you progress, choose other opportunities from this list to add to your life.

›› Closing Prayer

O God, you are God of the Sabbath. You commanded me to balance my life of activity with a life of rest and prayer. Give me the grace to do so. Amen.

Each Person Contributes to Salvation History

›› INTRODUCTION

Those who have seen their family tree or been involved in researching the identities of ancestors and ancestral homes find it both intellectually rewarding, and emotionally and spiritually fulfilling. People travel to a foreign country to meet distant relatives, see ancestral birthplaces, or rub crayons against the headstones of those whose blood runs in their veins. It is a taste of immortality, connecting you to the eons of life that existed before you and which, through the miracle of evolution and grace, have resulted in you and will flow into the future through you.

The family of faith has a similar ancestral lineage: the communion of saints. Our spiritual genealogy contributes to who we are as God's beloved and how we live that out within the context of community. Just as some avoid tracing their family trees for fear of finding disreputable characters hanging on the limbs, Christians often miss spiritual markers on their tree of faith that point out lessons that could place life on earth in closer proximity to the reign of God.

This week, your journey will uncover some of the rocks upon which your faith is built. Don't be afraid.

›› SCRIPTURE

The Lord, the God of their ancestors, sent persistently to them by his messengers, because he had compassion on his people and his dwelling place. 2 CHRONICLES 36:15

›› REFLECTION

It's fun to look at old family photos. Sometimes, the shock of seeing yourself in a long dead relative you've never met can be disconcerting. It's easier to think you exist untouched or uninfluenced by those who have gone before you, especially those relatives whose lives have not been exemplary. It isn't pleasant to recognize in your words, actions or expressions a likeness to someone you don't admire or want to emulate. But nonetheless, there it is. The good news is that you can choose how you will or won't incorporate family traits into your own life. The choices you make build your unique contribution to the family tree.

The same can be said for faith. Each ancestor in faith had a unique relationship with God and contributed to the body of faith and the revelation of God through their choices. Their poor choices established a dynamic of evil and suffering, like the disobedience in the garden. Their good choices set in motion a paradigm of good, like Abraham's hospitality to the strangers. In all cases, God, the faithful and persistent covenant-keeper, provided opportunity and direction and left the choice to them.

You are now a living covenant-keeper of faith. Some day, you too will be an ancestor. It is your turn to choose good over evil; to follow the light and not the darkness; to keep and not break your baptismal vows. You, too, have a unique contribution to make to the salvation history of those who follow you. What will it be?

>> Family Tree

Eve ate an apple and Sarah laughed
    Noah commanded a zoo.
Jacob loved Joseph most of all
    and fathered Israel, too.
Moses parted the raging seas
    lamented the golden calf;
Barefoot before the burning bush
    he brought the covenant plaques back.
Laws and rules, judges and kings,
    Ruth stayed by Naomi's side.
David sang psalms,
    his holy roots deep,
    sinning before he was saved.
Prophets lamented,
    "Repent and be saved!
    Accept God's mercy and love!"
Enter Mary,
    the Nazarene girl,
    pure in mind, body and soul.
Her choice to give birth
    brought Jesus to earth
    shed light in a dark, dark world.
His teaching and love
    healing and prayer
    brought God's reign closer yet.
His suffering and death
    led to new life
And his followers
    follow him still.

>> A Long Line of Spiritual Ancestors

One of the images that the storyteller in today's reading offers is that of a compassionate God who time and again warns people that they are straying from their covenant, that they are making poor choices that will result in sad consequences. When have you experienced God warning you to turn away from a poor choice? How has God shown you that you were straying from your covenant? Use your Bible to help you see your own spiritual history.

›› Reflection/Journal Writing

Reflect on your ancestors in faith. Who are the people whose approach to God invite your imitation? Who are the people, living or dead, famous or not, who turn your heart toward God? Who are those whose journey to stay faithful to the covenant inspires your own? Write down their names, and bless them as you do.

_____

_____

_____

_____

_____

_____

›› Action

Imagine that your community of faith is writing your obituary years from now. What would they say is your spiritual legacy? What needs to change in your life in order for your spiritual legacy to be something of which you can be proud? Create an obituary that reveals who God calls you to be and place it where it can motivate you to be that person each day.

›› Closing Prayer

All you angels and saints of God, mothers and fathers in faith, lift me up and empower me to create a living legacy of the Spirit, in Jesus' name. Amen.

Hate Darkness, Love the Light

>> INTRODUCTION

Young children often are afraid of the dark. They must be cajoled to bed with a light left burning through the night. They imagine beasts and ghosts and all manner of harmful and unhappy creatures roaming in the dark. But the night-light is enough to cast a spell of security and peace. They intuitively sense that the light has power over the dark.

Today's reflection leads you into the realm of darkness with the calm assurance that the light is more powerful. It invites you to acknowledge the presence of evil and your freedom to reject it, because you are a "child of the light."

>> SCRIPTURE

And this is the judgment, that the light has come into the world, and people loved darkness rather than light because their deeds were evil.
JOHN 3:19

>> REFLECTION

Evil is a term that stirs up apocalyptic images. People think of evil as the devil in a red cape, complete with pitchfork. They distance themselves from the real evil in the world and in their own lives by making it into a cartoon character, or something so monumentally beyond the average human's experience that it is inconceivable. Evil is the name people give to something Hitler did in those cremato-ria, or Stalin in labor camps. Evil loses its personal side because no one wants to admit that he or she is capable of choosing it.

Does someone choose evil because he is evil? What about the fact that God looked at all of creation and saw good? Evil exists when the covenant to be God's people, God's beloved, is broken. It exists because idols are shinier than living each day on purpose, or discerning and following God's will. Evil exists because there are people who want to "play" God and control life. Evil exists when those who know better are silent in its presence.

Jesus is the light of the world. He enables you to understand what is true and good. Evil doesn't have a chance if you stand in the light of Christ.

>> Bring on the Light

If darkness
    Did not exist
You could not recognize
    The light.
In the darkness,
    You are blind
    Fearful
    Groping for direction
At the darkest spot
    An act of faith
    Brings on the light
And the Light
    Scatters the darkness
    And fear
And reveals your holy purpose.

›› Ways to Identify Evil

When God created humanity, all humans were equal, good, and worthy of God's love. God's command was to love and anything that detracts from love or denies love is evil, sinful. Do you recognize evil? Here are some ways in which you can identify it:

• One person abusing another verbally, physically, or emotionally
• Any form of discrimination: racism, sexism, ageism, and the like
• People living in substandard housing
• Gossip that harms a person's reputation
• Exclusion rather than inclusion
• Domination of a person or group by another person or group
• Violence
• Disrespect for the dignity of each person
• Anything that opposes life or vitality
• Silence in the face of injustice or any of the items above.

›› Reflection/Journal Writing

Light a candle to assure your safety as you reflect on your encounters with evil. Use the ways to identify evil to name how evil has infiltrated your life. Perhaps it is an attitude or behavior of your own. It might be something within a group to which you belong. Write your thoughts and feelings and invite the light of Christ to illuminate ways in which you can defeat it.

_____

_____

_____

_____

_____

_____

›› ACTION

Determine to make candles a significant part of your spiritual and family life. Light a candle at mealtime and before you pray. Remind yourself and others that where two or three gather in Christ's name, in peace and respect, Jesus is present. When you go to church this week, light a candle as a prayer for the destruction of evil wherever it is present.

›› CLOSING PRAYER

As you light your prayer candle, sing this song:

This little light of mine, I'm gonna let it shine.
This little light of mine, I'm gonna let it shine.
This little light of mine, I'm gonna let it shine.
Let it shine, let it shine, let it shine.

The Gift of Faith

›› INTRODUCTION

Today you have to give up trying to convince God that you are worthy or unworthy. Today you have to face the fact that it is God's generosity and love that has initiated whatever spiritual inclinations, beliefs, and commitments you are able to make. Today you must decide to put away, once and for all, any claim to deserving the spiritual gifts you have been given.

Faith is a gift of God, free for all to claim. Eternal life has already been restored to you through Christ's gift of his life, death, and resurrection. Neither is based on the worthiness, intelligence, stewardship, or hard work of the receiver. Neither discriminates between those who are pure in mind, heart, or soul and those who are not. We are all sinners and salvation is free—a difficult reality to understand and accept in a world with so many strings. Do you believe it?

›› SCRIPTURE

For by grace you have been saved through faith…this is not your own doing; it is the gift of God, not the result of works. EPHESIANS 2:8–9

›› REFLECTION

Gifts are peculiar things. You love to receive them but then feel the need to do something to show appropriate appreciation. But what do you do when the giver is God and the gift is eternal life? It doesn't seem anything could top that. Yet for some reason, people try.

Even though God has made it clear that salvation comes through faith and not good works, you do everything in your power to prove your worthiness. Going to church, making charitable donations, helping the needy, acts of kindness, and the like become ways to show you are worthy of salvation. Good works, instead of being the fruit of our relationship with God, become the means to be accepted by God. The whole thing smacks of a lack of faith!

Do you or do you not believe that you were saved through the blood of Jesus Christ? Do you or do you not believe that God's graciousness is beyond what any human can imagine? Do you or do you not believe that God loves you so abundantly that you are not required to do anything except return that love? Do you or do you not believe that the love and free gifts of faith and salvation extended to you are extended to all of creation? It's hard to break through the American work ethic of independence: everything good you want to achieve depends on you—there's no free lunch. You win at the cost of someone else losing.

Well, with God, breakfast, lunch, and dinner are free from your effort, with one exception: accepting the gift you've been given.

>> Jesus Has Paid the Price

Nothing is free anymore;
    everything has a price tag.
Kids that once helped elderly neighbors from kindness
    now charge whatever they can get.
Companies that used to honor loyal employees
    now downsize at the first hint of profit.
Workers who would give their all to the same company
      for fifty years
    now jump ship at the first chance of a bigger salary.
Nothing is free.

National and state parks are almost unaffordable;
>   a cup of coffee costs more than a haircut;
>   chores that help the family maintain order
>   are reaching minimum wage status.
Nothing is free—
>   except the grace of God
>   faith
>   salvation in Jesus Christ.
Jesus has already paid the price
>   our price is gratitude
>   our price is love of God, self and others;
Our price is to give back—
>   freely,
>   no strings attached.

›› God's Generosity

There is something about human pride that causes us to resent being lumped in the same portfolio with everyone else. People don't want to be thrown in with beggars and killers and liars and cheats. If God's love is so universally available to everyone, no matter what, does it make it less important for you? Do you feel less special? If everyone's salvation has been purchased through Christ's death, should you bother to be good? To do good? What do you believe about salvation through the free gift of faith?

›› Reflection/Journal Writing

In addition to the gifts of faith and salvation, what other gifts has God freely given you that you could not earn?

_____

_____

_____

_____

_____

>> Action

Take one action today in imitation of God's free gifting. Offer at least one other person something that has no strings attached, something they cannot earn. Perhaps you will see a person who needs food walking or sitting on the street—take them to a meal. Perhaps a stray animal will show up at your door—bring them to the vet and pay the cost of their spaying. Perhaps you live close to a retirement center or nursing home—go there and ask to visit the person who never receives visitors. Today, give something to someone else that they do not ask for, cannot earn, do not expect and do not have to repay.

>> Closing Prayer

O God, I am overwhelmed by the vastness of your generosity. I do not know how to show my gratitude to Jesus for the price he paid for my eternal life. I am stymied. Thank you. Thank you. Thank you. Amen.

The Role of Good Works

›› INTRODUCTION

Yesterday you reflected on the fact that faith and salvation are free gifts of God and nothing you do will earn them for you. Today, you will focus on the role that good works play in the lives of those who accept faith in Christ and live out their salvation in the world.

If you are already saved, is that it? Can you do anything you want and it won't matter? Sorry! That's not how it works. The issue at stake is not the generous and merciful way that God chooses to act in your regard, but the way in which you respond to that action, how you use the gifts God has given you to live out your mission and purpose, the ongoing mission of Jesus.

›› SCRIPTURE

For we are what He has made us, created in Jesus Christ for good works, which God prepared beforehand to be our way of life.
EPHESIANS 2:10

›› REFLECTION

You are what God has made you: created in Jesus Christ for good works. Isn't this a fantastic statement? But wait, there's more: God prepared this structure to be your way of life. Is the purpose of your life becoming any clearer?

Paul tells the Ephesians that the purpose of life is "planted" within. It's not something you need to search the highways and byways to find. It's not something alien to you. You need look no further than your inner life and your outer behavior, your spirit and soul and your good works to understand the nature and purpose of your life and evaluate how well you are fulfilling it.

Good works are the outward fruit of a life of faith, freely given and accepted. Doing good in the world is not to be an exception to the rule of your life—it *is* the rule; it *is* your life. The compassion you feel for victims of natural disasters and the generosity of time, money, and talent you offer to aid them is the natural overflow of the need to do good that is part of being made in God's image.

Good works are the fruit of a faith that has vitality. Scripture tells us that the trees that don't produce will be cut down and burned because they are not fulfilling their purpose. It's a warning you have a chance to heed.

›› A Way of Life

Flowers bloom or not
    because it's their nature.
Animals bear young
    because that's how their species survives.
God gives
    because God doesn't know any other way
        to reveal God's self.
What about you?
    Are you bearing fruit?
    Is your life adorned with good works?
    Is your faith more than lip-service and public worship?
Why do you give?

›› Good Works Evaluation 101

It's time to evaluate whether or not the reflection and prayer of the past few weeks is bearing good fruit. Keep in mind that the reason you reflect is to understand, and the reason you try to understand is so that you can act. Today you'll evaluate how well you are moving toward faith that takes action.

On this Evaluation 101 page, list each and every good work you have accomplished since your forty days of renewal began. It's not bragging, nor is it meant to humiliate if you haven't done much. It's an opportunity to get a clear picture of how well you are moving out of your head and heart and into being Christ's hands and feet. List anything, small or large: whenever you offered a random act of kindness, visited a lonely person, sent a card of comfort, made a plan to tithe ten percent of your income to those in need, sold excess goods and gave the proceeds to a charitable cause—anything!

_____

_____

_____

_____

_____

_____

_____

_____

_____

_____

›› Reflection/Journal Writing

How do you feel after that last exercise? Are you pleased that the tree of your faith life is bearing good and lasting fruit? Do you see an ongoing and regular harvest? Or are you uncomfortable because you smell smoke and have visions of an approaching tree trimmer? Take some time to write about the "reality" of your life of good works. Is it a habit of your soul yet? What do you need to do in order for the purpose of your life to come front and center?

_____

_____

_____

_____

_____

›› Action

One of the hardest "good works" to undertake is what Scripture refers to as tithing. Those who know about financial stewardship teach that each household should be tithing ten percent of its total income to charity. Do a quick math calculation and see where your household falls. Discuss with your family how you could increase your stewardship of treasure by at least one percent annually until you reach ten percent. Discuss where these funds might do the best good work during this year. Draw up a commitment form and a plan for how each person's income will be placed in the fund. Share with each other what freedom or resistance you feel with this action.

›› Closing Prayer

Jesus, I want to bear fruit, fruit that will last and bring glory to your name. Show me the way of good works. Grant me the freedom and generosity of the children of God. Amen.

Blessed Are the Merciful

>> INTRODUCTION

One of the good works people have difficulty dispensing is mercy. Even though Jesus preaches that those who are merciful will be blessed, people shrink from offering mercy. What about justice? What about taking the consequence for your misdeeds? There seems to be an unwritten law that says only wimps give mercy!

In reality, mercy is for the strong, for those who know God, for those who don't need harshness and cruelty, spitefulness or callousness to shore up their weakness or fear. Mercy comes from those who believe God is merciful and who know their own need for God's mercy. God is rich in mercy. That should tell you something!

>> SCRIPTURE

God, who is rich in mercy…made us alive in Christ. EPHESIANS 2:4–5

>> REFLECTION

Mercy is an "old" word. You hear it most often in terms like "the prisoner asked for mercy." The word has almost a negative connotation in a country such as ours, where harsh punishment is the norm and cries for justice are loud.

Yet mercy is the opposite of justice. Mercy demands that justice be set aside, that you don't get the punishment you deserve but the love and forgiveness that you need. Where the human eye sees guilt and responds with a call for punishment, God sees the death of Jesus, who already paid the punishment. Jesus' death allows God to offer mercy.

God's mercy exists as the healing of guilt. It frees you from your sin, but it doesn't give you a license to sin. Mercy recognizes your repentance and asks you to be more and to give mercy to those who have wronged you. God's mercy is in endless supply, new every day. God's mercy endures forever.

›› GOD'S MERCY

When Jesus said
    be merciful,
    he wasn't talking about
       forgiving murderers,
       torturers,
       and terrorists—
    was he?
If you give mercy, does that mean
    crimes shouldn't be punished?
Does it mean
    you must forget the pain and heartache
    caused by others?
Why, why would God require mercy
    from those who belong to God?
Granting mercy to those who don't deserve it,
    as God does for you,
    gives freedom and peace to those
    who offer it.
Perhaps that is God's greatest mercy.

›› Practicing Mercy

Jesus taught that to obtain mercy one needs to be merciful. For each of the following situations, name a merciful response you could give:

• Your employer passes you over for a deserved promotion.
• Your children disobey your rules and get into trouble.
• A friend betrays your trust.

›› Reflection/Journal Writing

Mercy is also known as kindness, compassion, leniency, and benevolence. Can you find at least one of these qualities in yourself? Which of them would apply most easily to you? Which do you struggle to demonstrate to yourself and others? Write about the quality of mercy in your life and what you need to increase your ability to "be merciful as your heavenly Father is merciful."

_____

_____

_____

_____

_____

›› Action

Go out today with the intention of showing mercy to those you meet. Stretch yourself to refrain from judgment, from any form of retaliation or punishment.

›› Closing Prayer

Merciful God, you are full of empathy, thoughtfulness and compassion. I pray for a heart like yours, O God, rich in mercy and abounding in kindness. Amen.

Holy Citizenship

›› Introduction

As this fourth week of reflection and habit changing draws to an end, Paul reminds you that you are part of the family of God. You are a member of the band of disciples who follow Christ. You are among the saints, a citizen of the city of God. This comes with responsibilities and offers rewards. Today, take time to rejoice in the gift of holy citizenship.

›› Scripture

So then you are no longer strangers and sojourners, but you are fellow citizens with the holy ones and members of the household of God.
Ephesians 3:19

›› Reflection

Have you ever been to a foreign country? What was your experience like? People who travel to other countries are aware of the uneasiness of not understanding the language, of customs that are unfamiliar, and foods that are exotic and unusual. Yet in the midst of new sights, sounds, and occurrences, travelers realize that there are qualities common to the human race, everywhere in the world. On the other hand, they grow in understanding of the differences.

In some countries, citizens are not allowed to express their political opinions if they differ from those in power. Some citizens are not allowed to worship the God of their choice. Some have very liberal welfare systems; some have no government benefits. In most societies, there is a system of classes with the wealthier and better connected citizens getting more of the economic resources and extra benefits. Some societies are built on violence; others are pacifist. In all cases, those who choose to remain citizens agree to live with the rules of their society. They learn to work, pray, love and survive within those rules.

What about citizens within God's city? What is that like?

>> THE CITY OF GOD

People are equal here.
There are no gender disputes
    no racial antagonism
    no inequalities of any sort.
Everyone bows to the other's need.
There are no grudges
    no violence
    no fear.
The city of God
    is available to all;
    unrestricted access
        gives everyone the same chance.
No one feels out of place;
    there are no strangers,
    no labels that separate.

>> A SOBER EVALUATION

As you reflect on the beauty and harmony of citizenship in the holy city of God, you need to compare it to the city you live in now. Read a major paper in your region. Make four columns on a sheet of paper. Label the first: Global, the second: National, the third:

State, and the fourth: Local. As you read, list the issues you see in each area that are not in line with the reign of God.

›› Reflection/Journal Writing

Write about the responsibilities and rewards that are yours because you are a citizen of the city of God. What do you realize? What can you do about it?

_____

_____

_____

_____

_____

_____

›› Action

Your baptism sent you forth to transform this secular "city," the world, into the city of God. It gave you the spiritual mandate and strength to be a leaven, a citizen who could and must align your world with God's reign. Choose one of the issues you identified in your reading and determine a way to improve it, as a good citizen of both the world and God's city. Don't stop at thinking; act!

›› Closing Prayer

God, you rule the sun and stars. Your will rotates the earth and gives me life. I offer you my loyalty above all other rulers. I claim your law above all others. Amen.

Change Requires Patience

>> INTRODUCTION

Patience is a virtue. This has become a trite comeback most often used when someone is not exhibiting patience. The fact is that patience as a virtue is a habit. It's a way of showing God's life in situations that are trying. And one of the situations that try people most is coping with change.

Unfortunately, change is a constant in life. It is always happening, and little is under individual control. However, with patience and the willingness to work toward positive solutions that reflect God's call for peace, even change can produce results beyond the expected. Today, reflect on the virtue of patience and how God wants you to use it to change your life.

>> SCRIPTURE

…the blind receive their sight, the lame walk, lepers are cleansed, the deaf hear, the dead are raised, and the poor have good news brought to them. LUKE 7:19–23

›› REFLECTION

John the Baptist was all about change. He preached, perhaps even harangued, anyone within earshot about the need to change, to repent, in order to receive the Messiah. John was no stranger to change nor did he fear it. He was so adamant that Herod should change his immoral ways that he was put into jail. But John had a preconceived notion about what change would look like.

When John met Jesus, it confirmed the focus of his life. Here was the Messiah. Here was the one on whom his belief and life had been built. Surely now, the changes John preached and for which he suffered, would come to be. Surely, now.

But as John languished in prison, he became impatient. He wanted the Messiah to do what John expected him to do. As time went on, he began to doubt the Messiah. Finally, he sent his own followers to ask Jesus if he really was the one who was going to change the world and save Israel. John's patience was at an end and he needed reassurance in order to persevere.

Jesus' message shows John that the change the Messiah brings is healing, that changing people's hearts and minds and returning them to God will not come about through violence and fear, but over time, through patience and healing. Jesus knew the anguish of John's soul, and his words are sent as a balm and as a source of courage. Jesus wants John, and you, to know that even as you wait patiently, or impatiently, for change to occur in your life, God, through Jesus is already bringing it about.

›› GIVE ME PATIENCE, NOW

What I want, God,
    I want now.
I know what is best for my soul
    so give it to me now.
I know the answer to this dilemma
    so make it happen now.

I'm sure of the path my life should take
    so take away the obstacles, now.
Now, now, now—
    if only I could wait
    and trust
        that God will show the way
        that God knows what my life needs
        that God is working in the midst of my impatience
            to produce everything that will speak to God's glory.
Give me patience, now!

›› Change

Change takes patience because it usually involves changing a habit. You have been engaged in change over the past several weeks. It hasn't always been easy, and perhaps you've not done as well as you hoped. Yet you are here today, and the message is to be patient with yourself and realize that the change God is trying to evoke is your healing.

- What is the healing that you are most aware of needing in your life?
- What change would be involved if you were healed?
- Are you ready to wait on the Lord to heal you?
- Are you willing to accept the change your healing will bring?

›› Reflection/Journal Writing

Your life has witnessed many changes over the years. Use your writing time today to notice those that brought healing and those that brought more pain. Was there something that was present or missing that caused the difference? What has been your normal response to change? Is there anything you need to do in order to alter that response to one which is more receptive to God's activity in your life?

_____

_____

_____

_____

_____

_____

›› ACTION

Consider signing up as a reading tutor for an adult who cannot read, or as a volunteer for the blind or disabled. Seek out situations where your greatest gift will be the gift of patience and use the opportunity to grow in this virtue.

›› CLOSING PRAYER

Jesus, Lord of all who call to you in need of healing, hear my impatient voice. Place your healing hands on me, show me where I am deaf, lame, and blind, and call me forth into wholeness as you gift me with the patience to await your sacred touch. Amen.

Jesus Is Calling You

›› INTRODUCTION

Do you consider yourself a courageous person? Are you able to stand strong in situations that call for bravery? Do you try to escape the notice of others or are you willing to express your needs and wants with determination? Do you persevere in the face of obstacles?

Blind Bartimaeus is no longer content to be on the fringes of life. He wants the fullness of life that he hears all around him. When he meets Jesus, he senses that this is where he will find it. It takes courage to ask for what he wants and perhaps be rejected. Yet Bartimaeus takes the chance. As you move toward the last ten days of fulfilling your covenant, take time to evaluate your own courage.

›› SCRIPTURE

Courage,…get up, he is calling you. MARK 10:49

›› REFLECTION

Translations differ on the healing of Bartimaeus, the blind beggar. One has the apostles telling Bartimaeus to have "courage," when Jesus calls him to come forward. Another says, "take heart." Either way, the message is clear. Bartimaeus, whose blindness kept him by the side of the road, calls out and asks for mercy when he hears

Jesus and the crowd. Though others tell him to be quiet, he pursues what he needs. Jesus hears him and calls him to come forward. Bartimaeus bundles up his courage to answer the call and when Jesus asks him what he wants, Bartimaeus asks to see again. He is healed and the text says that "immediately he…followed him on the way" (Mark 10:52).

What can you learn here about your own journey, your call from the Lord? First of all, your decision to move off of the roadside of your spiritual life and into the crowd surrounding Jesus has placed you in the position of getting what you say you want: a deeper spiritual life, a life lived on purpose. Now, Jesus calls you to come forward, to present your needs and boldly express what it is you want God to do for you. He shows you that what you want will involve God's healing and when you have received it, your task is to follow Christ. Are you ready to hear the words of healing and to step forward, "on the way?"

›› Sight For the Blind

Blindness
  is not only a loss of physical sight;
    it can be a loss of spiritual sight as well.
It's possible to lose sight
  of what and who is important
  of how life is leading toward
    or away from your true self.
Spiritual blindness can be healed
  one hundred percent of the time;
  but it takes courage.
It takes a heart that knows
  what it wants and needs.
It takes trusting the voice of Jesus
  and not those who scoff
Bartimaeus was given a chance to be healed.
He took it and danced along the way.

›› A Spiritual Eye Exam

What does it take to see clearly, in the spiritual life? It takes:
• A pure heart
• An honest self-evaluation
• Courage
• A sincere desire to be united with God
• Faith and trust in Jesus Christ
• An attitude of prayer flowing from the Word of God.

›› Reflection/Journal Writing

What is your heart's desire? What do you really want God to do for
you? What is it that keeps you by the roadside in your spiritual life,
unable to live it fully? What would it take to have the courage to
move toward Jesus and accept his healing? Today's writing is an
important step in moving forward from reflection to discipleship—don't skip over it.

_____

_____

_____

_____

_____

›› Action

After you've finished the reflection today, make an appointment
with either a spiritual director to talk about what it is you want
God to do in your life, and/or a priest, for confession. Take seri-
ously Jesus' call to come forward. Allow yourself to be healed and
the rest will come naturally.

›› Closing Prayer

Jesus, Son of David, have mercy on me so that I can follow you
with a joyful and grateful heart. Amen.

Walking the Disciple's Path

>> INTRODUCTION

Today we begin the countdown to the end of this covenant of renewal. You have worked hard to get this far and the end is in sight. The next eight days will reveal the path ahead, the path of discipleship. The steps you have taken so far have prepared you to take each of the next eight steps. On each of the next eight days, one step will be revealed and as you reflect on it, you will be moving forward to a final commitment of living on purpose for the rest of your life.

Today, you will reflect on an overview of the eight steps on the disciple's path. It's all about losing your life—not a thought most of us wish to engage—yet gaining the heart of a disciple's life.

>> SCRIPTURE

Whoever finds [his] life will lose it, and whoever loses [his] life for my sake will find it. MATTHEW 10:39

>> REFLECTION

Perhaps the most difficult step to take for those who wish to be disciples is the step of surrendering. Surrender means vulnerability. It means facing an unknown future where someone else is in control of your life. It means you are certain to find your life changed in ways you cannot imagine. When you surrender you submit, yield, lay down your weapons and relinquish your power.

The beauty of God's way is that it is only by surrendering to God's control that the deepest desires of the heart are met. To make surrender easier to understand and thus to accept, the next eight days will break it down into steps. Including today, take each step and ponder it. Perhaps it will take you more than one day to accomplish before you are ready to accept and act on that step. That's okay; take the time you need. At the end of these days, you will find My Commitment to Live as a Disciple (p. 154). If you have taken the steps you need to take, and if you decide to make that commitment, you will be ready to surrender for the rest of your life.

›› Admit Defeat

O God,
   you know me through and through
   you know my capabilities, my strengths
   you know my hesitations, my resistance.
You know, O God,
   how much I love to win
   how important my independence is
   how much I need to control my life.
Must I yield to your love
   in order to find peace
   in order to know the joy of intimacy with you?
Defeat me, O God
   I lay down my arms
   my heart
   my being.
I surrender to your love.

>> Tips on Surrendering

Because it isn't easy to walk the way of surrender, here are a few tips you can practice as you try to live this changed way of being.

- Before you stand your ground in an argument, consider giving in.
- Allow yourself to submit to the will of others in anything that isn't a matter of moral rightness, at least once each day.
- Admit when you are in over your head and ask for help.
- Review your "treasures" and part with them one at a time. (Keep in mind these are not necessarily things.)
- Pray the mantra, "Jesus, I am yours, do with me what you will."

>> Reflection/Journal Writing

Over the years you have probably experienced surrender, submission, and forfeiting your will for that of another. Were any of these done purely for love and without grumbling or resentment? Write about how love changed your surrender.

_____

_____

_____

_____

>> Action

Join a team or group where there is a task to accomplish and you are not in charge. Be sure to place yourself in a position where you will have to take, not give, direction. Follow your directions without debate or trying to improve on them. Offer up the discomfort this may cause you for the grace of learning to surrender.

>> Closing Prayer

Jesus, you surrendered your entire life to your Father because of love. You have shown me the way of surrender, now help me to follow it. Amen.

Step One on the Disciple's Path: Leave Your Nets

>> INTRODUCTION

This first step, built on a fishing metaphor, may seem vague to those for whom fishing is not a way of life. Yet the first followers of Jesus were simple fishermen, tending their nets. Their livelihood depended on how many fish they could catch and sell. Their families depended on their prowess and perseverance in all kinds of weather. Their success depended on the quality of their nets as much as on their own abilities. Fishermen spend huge amounts of time mending the holes in their nets. When they aren't fishing or selling, they are mending.

Today Jesus says to them and to you, if you want to walk the way with me, leave your nets.

>> SCRIPTURE

Come after me and I will make you fishers of [men]. Immediately they left their nets and followed him. MATTHEW 4:19–20

›› REFLECTION

Scripture tells us that Peter and Andrew left their nets immediately in order to follow Jesus. That sounds both impetuous and exhilarating. Have you ever wished that you could just step off the merry-go-round and do something else, something that seems more meaningful?

Throughout Scripture, those who follow Jesus are asked to leave what they have had as their focus in life and to refocus on Jesus. Think about it: the fishermen must leave their nets, Zacchaeus must get down from the tree and leave his tax collecting, the woman at the well must leave her "husband," the rich young man, his riches. Jesus even tells one wannabe disciple that he must leave his dead father for others to bury.

This seems a bit much to ask, doesn't it? Do you take the words "leave your nets" literally, or do you see the metaphor? The nets refer to your current way of life and all that it involves, especially that which forms a resistance to being a follower of Christ. If the net is work, then leave it behind "as you do it now." If the net is deception or manipulation, leave it. If the net is sin in your life, leave it. If the net is riches and things, leave them. If the net is people who do not understand or support your desire to follow Christ, leave them. This may seem harsh. It may seem impossible. Yet those who made a commitment to follow Jesus all had the same step to take. Scripture says some did so and some "went away sad." Which will you be?

›› FISHING FOR PEOPLE

Peter and Andrew,
> the first to be called
> but not the last.
What was it like to hear this rabbi
> speak of a new way of life?
Did you waver at all?

Did you consider the consequences
    of what you would give up?
What did your spouses think?
How did you care for your family?
We modern disciples
    want to fish;
    we can almost taste the catch.
But how can we leave behind
    the nets that occupy our time,
    that capture our lives,
    that others seem to depend on?
Immediately is too soon to start out—
    or is it?

›› LEAVE YOUR NETS

Sometimes the best way to leave your nets is to mend them, to alter them so that they are not an obstacle to following Christ, but an asset. If fishermen do not mend their nets, then the holes hinder their ability to catch fish. If nets are not fixable, however, then they must be left behind.

- Can you alter your work hours so that they don't consume your life but allow time for service to others?
- What about your attitude toward work? Can you see work as a means of helping others rather than simply a paycheck?
- Are your relationships freeing? Do they offer you strength and motivation to live your life on purpose or do they drag you down and focus you on things that do not serve the Lord's will?
- Have you confessed your sin yet? Have you mended your ways? Are you working on changing the patterns and choices that have kept you from the Lord?
- What else needs mending so that you can leave your nets behind?

›› Reflection/Journal Writing

A net can be a useful tool when it is mended and ready to be used in the hands of the fisherman. Or, it can be a cumbersome and tangled mess of lines that serves no purpose at all. Write about your nets and how God wants to use them to catch people.

_____

_____

_____

_____

_____

_____

›› Action

Write a prayer offering yourself to God, and include the nets you want to leave behind and the fish you want to catch. Address it to the Creator, Son, or Holy Spirit, and pray it for the rest of your journey of renewal.

›› Closing Prayer

Jesus, you stood on the shore and called. I've answered, "Here I am." Now you want me to leave behind all that stands in the way of following you and doing your will. Show me the way to leave my nets. Give me a vision of my new nets. Take the lead out of my feet so that I can follow you immediately. Amen.

Step Two on the Disciple's Path: Live As a Blessing

›› INTRODUCTION

If you are reading this page you have made it past step one. Your nets are now mended or in process, and you are eager to move forward toward full discipleship. Step two speaks about living a blessed life. Most of the time, when people talk about being blessed, they tell stories of good things happening in their lives. The blessings of disciples are definitely good, but are often wrapped in challenges. Today you reflect on whether you approach life as a blessing or curse, and, whether you are willing to choose life in the face of what others may see as a curse.

›› SCRIPTURE

Blessed are those who are poor in spirit...mourn...are meek...hunger and thirst for what is right...are merciful...are pure of heart...are peacemakers...are persecuted for the sake of what is right....Blessed are you when they insult you...persecute you...utter every kind of evil against you because of me.... MATTHEW 5:1–12

Jesus now has a band of followers and he is pursued by many people. They travel throughout Galilee teaching, healing and spreading the good news of God's love. Jesus is becoming famous, and as most followers of the famous, so are the disciples. It has reached a point where Jesus cannot go anywhere without meeting large crowds who want to hear him preach or be healed by his blessing.

Lest the disciples get caught up in the wrong interpretation, Jesus takes them to a quieter place and teaches them the real meaning of living a blessed life. It isn't what they expect. It doesn't say anything about fame or riches. It isn't the life they thought about when they left their nets. Yet Jesus is clear.

Living a blessed life, a life of purpose, involves gentleness not arrogance, purity of heart not internal discontent, grief, a deep desire to do the right thing even if the consequences are misunderstanding, persecution, or rejection. Living a blessed life means striving for peace and harmony, and always being ready to give generously. Jesus makes the way clear and the disciples are stunned. It sounds good—but will it put food on the table?

›› Life Is a Blessing

Blessed are you
> when you are gentle
> when your pride is under control
> > and you know to whom the glory belongs.

Blessed are you
> when you seek and offer peace
> when your relationships reek of peace
> > and you lead the way to nonviolence.

Blessed are you
> when your heart is clear in its purpose
> when you are not hindered by subterfuge
> > and your inner cleanliness shines in good works.

Blessed are you
>   when even the vilest of actions against you
>   cannot deter your spirit
> 	and the Lord is your rock and your shield.

›› Blessed Are You

Which of the beatitudes would someone else say is the most outstanding in your life? Which do you struggle to make a living attitude? Will you be able to live as a blessing for others? What might hold you back?

›› Reflection/Journal Writing

How are you blessed? Rewrite the beatitudes, interpreting them in the light of your own life. Express these blessings in a message for others that speaks of contemporary realities? For example, you might say, "Blessed are you when a small child forgives your impatience and loves you unconditionally," because you see this happening with your children.

_____

_____

_____

_____

_____

›› Action

Choose one of the beatitudes and make it an action today; if you can do more than one, great. But make it your goal to incorporate a new beatitude each day until you are a living beatitude that becomes a blessing for others.

›› Closing Prayer

Lord Jesus, I am blessed. I want to be a person with the right attitudes, one whose way of life is a blessing for self and others. Amen.

Step Three on the Disciple's Path: Love Your Enemies

>> INTRODUCTION

Okay, you've managed to leave your nets and resolve to live as a blessing. Step three is among the hardest tasks you will ever undertake: loving your enemies and those who try to harm you. Wow! This might be the deal breaker. But it doesn't have to be, because you have spent all these days shoring up your strength in Christ, trusting Christ to be there for you, turning over control to God's wisdom and responding to each call with a positive move forward. All these days have been preparing you for this moment: learning to love your enemies.

If you're one of the rare people who say you can't think of any enemies, there is no one you know who would harm you, then give thanks to God and move to the next step. But what if there are enemies? What if you've already been harmed and you know others who do not wish you well? What then? Can you still be a disciple?

But I say to you, love your enemies and do good to those who perse-cute you. MATTHEW 5:44

>> REFLECTION

Jesus was definitely someone who would never give his followers a task that he, himself, was unwilling to do. This is the sign of a good leader. Jesus asked his disciples to live a blessed life, and then he spelled out elements of that life in detail.

The disciples were probably doing okay until Jesus got to the part about loving their enemies. They were already aware of people in the crowds who did not like what Jesus was teaching. The Pharisees seemed eager to trick him into saying something blasphemous, and others accused him of trying to place himself in a position too close to God. Sometimes there was tension, and the disciples were aware that it could get worse. But were these people their enemies? Jesus treated them all the same. He answered their questions and didn't ridicule or argue with them. He didn't hide from their scrutiny, but talked openly and freely with all who came.

Then again, Samaritans were their natural enemies, and yet Jesus talked with a Samaritan woman as though she were a friend. He expected them to treat her with respect, as well. How could you love your enemies when they meant to harm you? How could you let someone like that into the fold of your trust? Shouldn't you defend yourself against those who would hurt you? It was a dilemma they didn't yet know how to face.

>> WHO IS THE ENEMY?

In today's world
    enemies are many.
Anyone who is different
    seems to wear the label
    enemy.

Different race? You are a potential enemy.
Different gender? You are a potential enemy.
Different religion? You are a potential enemy.
Different political affiliation? You are a potential enemy.
God who is all, in all
must wonder:
Is God an enemy, too?
What will happen, if you love your enemies?
What will happen if love is your defense against hate
and the heavy cross your shield against death?

›› Love Your Enemies

This step might take you some time to accept and act on. Take whatever time you need. Keep in mind these examples as you think about your own ability to change swords into plowshares and enemies into allies.

- If someone lies about you, go and ask for a conversation to bring out the facts.
- If someone rejects you, write a note thanking them for showing you that you could survive rejection.
- If someone harms your family or your family name, put their name(s) first on your prayer list and pray for their well-being.
- If someone physically abuses you, report the abuse to the proper authorities so that this person can get help.
- Keep in mind that God's wisdom is stronger than everything you may think foolish.

›› Reflection/Journal Writing

Reflect on the place of enemies in your life. Make a list, starting with your "worst" enemy at the top. What would it take you to show a loving gesture to this person? What actions could you take that would lower his or her defenses and turn him or her into a friend?

_____

_____

_____

_____

_____

_____

›› Action

During your reflection you identified your "enemies." Now is a chance to practice the life of a disciple, to swallow your instinct to defend yourself against them and instead, to reach out in peace. Write a letter (or make a phone call, if that works for you) to the one who sits at the top of your "enemy list."

›› Closing Prayer

O God, you are God of peace and good will. You came to offer us peace and the fullness of life. Help me to reach out to my enemies and to make them my allies. Assist me in becoming like you in all things. Amen.

Step Four on the Disciple's Path: Give for the Right Reasons

>> Introduction

If you've made it to step four, you are solidly on the disciple's path. Today you look at giving. The reading tells you to give for the right reasons, but what are the right reasons? Remember the Pharisee and the widow? Both gave, but one gave from his excess and in a grand way, so that others would know how much he gave. The widow gave from her need, quietly, from her heart. She gave under duress. Jesus says that her gift was more acceptable, more pleasing to God. Today's reading makes the same point, and it is an especially important one for those who would be disciples because it has a special twist of meaning that goes far beyond how much one gives.

>> Scripture

Take care not to perform righteous deeds in order that people may see them....But when you give...do not let your right hand know what your left hand is doing. MATTHEW 6:1–3

>> REFLECTION

In Mark's version of the widow's mite, the story comes just after Jesus has chastised those who make a practice of cheating widows out of the little they have, who have no sensitivity to their need and instead prey on their vulnerability (Mark 12:40). When Jesus is finished speaking, he sits down opposite the offering box, and studies the temple activity. In doing so he sees the two small coins the widow offers. His praise of her is a warning to those who cheat her and a temple that causes a person in her situation to have to put the little she has into their coffers or not be allowed to pray. Mark states that Jesus never goes to the temple again.

In this reading from Matthew, Jesus' teaching about almsgiving comes in a long section of many teachings that are part of the section on proclaiming the kingdom. These teachings show what it will take to be a follower of Christ, to be a witness to the good news. Giving for the right reasons—not because others will see and give praise, and not because one is forced to do so, but from the heart, with a good conscience and from love of God—is the only way to proclaim the values of God's reign. Disciples have a twofold mission in relation to giving: they should give generously, out of love; and they should be sensitive to the needs of others, not imposing requirements that cause them suffering in order to pursue their relationship with God.

One has to do with how you take care of your personal giving; the other, how you structure your pastoral care of others.

>> THE WIDOW'S TREASURE

Being a widow is a trial,
> especially if you are poor or just getting by
> or don't have children
>> to care for you and see that your needs are met.

Widows look to God
　　for who else is there
　　who empathizes and stands ready to help?
Widows look to their place of faith
　　for comfort and support
　　for a safe place in which to caress their cares.
In some places, widows are invisible
　　they've lost their standing;
　　only their financial donations enable them to be counted.
There are those who prey on the vulnerable
　　who cheat those they think won't know or notice
　　who demand more of those who have little
　　who make no exceptions and offer no mercy.
Not so with Jesus.
His good news embraces the widow and the orphan,
　　all those whose place in the world has been jeopardized.
And not so with those who follow Christ.

›› With a Trumpet Blast or in Secret?

Make a list of the various ways in which you give of your time, talent, and treasure. Next to each, list whether this is given in ways all can see or in secret, between you and God.

›› Reflection/Journal Writing

Do you give of your time, talent and treasure out of obligation or out of love? Are you more like the Pharisee or the widow? Take a closer look at your relationship to giving and write what your heart sees.

_____

_____

_____

_____

_____

>> Action

In previous reflections, you confronted the issue of tithing as a way to help you remember that the Lord is the source of all blessings. In keeping with your desire to give for the right reasons, when you make a donation to your church or charity, make a conscious connection to a specific blessing God has given you. For example, "I give this donation in thanksgiving for the health of my family."

Observe the way in which the widows, the poor, the strangers are treated in your church. Do the structures and expectations make it more difficult for them to offer themselves without undo hardship? Are they welcome just as they are, even if unable to give? Get involved in establishing a community attitude and action where all are welcome without regard to their monetary or social status.

>> Closing Prayer

O God, your generosity knows no bounds. You give without counting the cost yet you do not compare the gifts of those you love. Create in us hearts filled with compassion and generosity; hearts that seek nothing except to give you praise. Amen.

Step Five on the Disciple's Path: Pray Like Jesus

>> Introduction

Prayer is the pathway of long-term discipleship. It is through a life of prayer that service is balanced and the disciple is able to keep a clear vision. Prayer is food for the soul. Prayer gave Jesus the stamina to seek and follow God's will, the compassion to love his enemies, the courage to face the cross. Prayer is the mantra you hold in your heart throughout the day, and the last words to leave your lips. Today, Jesus teaches his disciples the difference between genuine prayer that pleases God and prayer that is pious lip-service. Do you know the difference?

>> Scripture

When you pray, do not babble like the pagans....Your Father knows what you need before you ask him. Matthew 6:7–8

This is how you are to pray: Our Father.... Matthew 6:9–15

›› REFLECTION

Prayer takes a lot of trust. After all, if you believe that God already knows what you need, why bother to ask? Yet Jesus never failed to go to God in prayer. He didn't just pray when times were difficult and he was looking for guidance and relief, such as in the garden before his death. Jesus prayed after spending time in preaching and teaching. He prayed alone and with others. He prayed at meals. He prayed silently and aloud, with authority. He also taught his disciples how to pray. He taught them not to babble on as though God didn't have a clue, but to praise God, make known your needs as you see them, and then let God use you to accomplish God's will.

If you look closely at the Our Father, certain elements stand out: one is personal relationship—but one that is shared with others. Another is praise. Another is a call for God's will and presence to become clear and pervasive. Another is a request for what you need, a request for forgiveness and the ability to forgive, and for protection against yielding to what is not of God. Does this look like your prayer?

›› CONVERSING WITH GOD

The disciples prayed in the temple,
    they prayed at their Sabbath table;
    they were good Jews.
But Jesus taught them something else:
    that God is in a personal relationship,
    that God is always available and approachable
        just like a parent whose love does not end.
The disciples prayed the formula prayers
    with their rituals and gestures.
Jesus taught them something else:
    that praising God from your heart is a psalm of love
    that God knows without your words or gestures
        what is best for each of the beloved.

Prayer was the food of Jesus' soul;
>   his body and blood became prayer,
>   food for all who would follow him,
>   nourishment for each soul.

›› Shaping Your Prayer

Shape your prayer today based on the formula of the Our Father, as shown in today's reflection. What words might you use to call upon God, following Jesus' words? As a practical reminder, review this checklist:

- Do you have a place for your daily prayer and reflection?
- Is it comfortable enough to support your spirit but not to distract you?
- Is it quiet, a place where you can center and focus?
- Do you begin with deep breathing and becoming conscious of God's presence? (Perhaps you may want to go back and review the centering technique on p. 18.)
- Are your Bible and any other resources easily available?
- Do you have a plan for when and how you can pray throughout the day?

›› Reflection/Journal Writing

Use this time today to write about the role prayer plays in your life. Describe how you were taught to pray and whether it differs from how you pray now. How does your prayer life affect the rest of your life? Listen as God tells you how God would like you to pray.

_____

_____

_____

_____

_____

_____

›› Action and Closing Prayer

When you have some time to spend today, say the Lord's Prayer, and take an hour to do it. Too often we speed through this familiar prayer and wonder why its power fails to convert us. Instead, use this prayer in an act of contemplation, slowly and meditatively lingering on each word and phrase. What does it mean to say, "Our" Father? Is Father a word for God to which you relate or is another image of God more personal? Let each phrase speak to you personally.

Step Six on the Disciple's Path: See the Good

›› INTRODUCTION

To judge is like taking sides. You have to make up your mind about an issue. You consider the facts and then determine an appropriate conclusion. When you judge you make a decision or give an opinion or verdict, and you are generally looking for what is wrong with the person or situation. In civil society, judges are generally held in high esteem—that is, until they make a ruling that doesn't please someone or that seems to go beyond the boundaries of their authority or expertise. Judges are considered experts, authorities, and final arbiters.

It's one thing to have an opinion and to make a decision about the events affecting your own life; another when you judge the worth or character of others. Perhaps this is why Jesus was so adamant about his disciples not setting themselves up in judgment of others, but rather, looking for the good.

>> SCRIPTURE

The measure with which you measure will be measured out to you.
MATTHEW 7:2

Remove the wooden beam from your eye first; then you will see clearly to remove the splinter from your brother's eye. MATTHEW 7:5

>> REFLECTION

Jesus couldn't be clearer. He tells his disciples not to judge. Period. He expands this somewhat by explaining that those who judge will have the same yardstick applied to them. Imagine, whatever opinion or critique or assessment you make of someone else is the same one by which you will be evaluated. That's scary for all but the purest of followers.

Jesus didn't take sides. What he did was to invite those he encountered to choose life, unity with others, peace and harmony within, and genuine goodness in service to others. Refusing to take sides doesn't mean refusing to stand for something. Jesus stood for faithfulness to the kingdom of God. He refused to condemn and left open the door for change and for a response to grace. Jesus saw the innate goodness in each person and realized that God's unconditional love would find a place within each person when each found his or her own inner goodness to live out of.

Today's reading invites you to recognize that every person has a past, present, and future, including you. It implies that if God judged you, your "sin" would be greater than what you now see in others. Not only can you not love another if you don't love yourself; but if you judge another, it can only be with the same yardstick you use to judge yourself. Most wouldn't want to be put to that test.

It does no good to dwell on the past, except as a way to change things for the better and to pave a way to the future. This is a habit of the soul that needs attention.

>> Yardsticks for the Spirit

How do you measure the soul?
Is there a ruler that can mark off its depth or
gauge its goodness?
Is what you see really all there is?
Is that the standard you want used when you are judged,
only what your actions demonstrate or
your words betray?
What about what was in your heart?
What about the intention that was lost?
What about the feelings that were never expressed?
How do you measure the goodness of a person?
Is there only one way that tells the whole story?
God's measure is Christ,
in whom you live and move and have life.
God's measure is unending opportunities
to make the right choices,
to be who it is you already are.
How do you measure the soul of another?
With the same yardstick you want used on your own:
God's mercy and love.

>> A Way to Measure

Create a new measuring rod by which you assess both your own
actions as a disciple and the actions of those you meet. Use the
eight steps on the disciple's path as a start. Draw a picture or write
down your thoughts, and keep it as a bookmark in your Bible or
by your nightstand. Use this measuring rod with your examen at
night or your morning prayer.

>> Reflection/Journal Writing

Are you an encouraging or judgmental person? Are you quicker to
criticize or to praise? Do you find yourself finding fault with oth-

ers or affirming the good in them? Write about your attitudes and what you like or dislike.

_____

_____

_____

_____

_____

_____

>> ACTION

Apologize to anyone whom you have criticized, judged, or taken sides against in the past week. Swallow your pride, and as an act of humility, approach the person with your apology. Explain why you are apologizing and try to cite at least one positive aspect of that person's life that you praise God for.

>> CLOSING PRAYER

Gentle Lord, brother to all, you accepted people as they were and didn't take sides against them. Even Judas was treated as your brother as you held out the invitation to change right to the very end. Give me a nonjudgmental spirit that I may draw others to God, as you did. Amen.

Step Seven on the Disciple's Path: Heal All You Meet

›› Introduction

In the course of the past thirty-eight days, you've had the opportunity to consider the broken areas of your life and how you might work toward wholeness or healing. Some of these areas involved your relationships with others or the way in which your brokenness affected others. Most of the emphasis, however, was on you. During these days of journey on the path to discipleship and finding your purpose in life, the emphasis has been on how you offer others what God has given you, in Christ. Today, you look at healing others. Yes, you can be a healer and your gift of healing can lead others to glorify God. Learn how from the Master.

›› Scripture

I will come and cure him. Matthew 8:7

He touched her hand and the fever left her. Matthew 8:15

Stand up, take your bed and go to your home. Matthew 9:7

›› REFLECTION

The Scripture references to healing are too numerous to count. You find them in the most obvious stories of physical healing and in the more subtle tales of spiritual awakening and conversion. What permeates all of the healing images is that they take place within the ordinary events of everyday life. A child or friend is sick, a mother-in-law is dying, a paralyzed man comes to the house, beggars call out beside the road, a woman is condemned for her faith or her lifestyle or her disease, a family is embarrassed by running out of wine, groups of people are shunned and discriminated against, a friend lies or betrays: the stuff of life presents the opportunity to heal.

Jesus seems never to have missed or refused an opportunity to heal. He could have said he was too tired after walking so many miles and preaching to so many people; or he was too busy doing God's work; or he just wasn't in the mood. Instead, he went about his daily life and where he met a person who needed a touch, a word of affirmation, an understanding heart, nonjudgmental acceptance, forgiveness, welcome or simply presence—he gave it. When he felt depleted by the giving, he went to a quiet place and prayed to be filled for another day. And then he gave again. The miracle of Jesus' healing is not in the wholeness of body, mind, or spirit experienced by others, but in the realization that he told his disciples to go and do the same in his name.

You have the power to heal yourself and others, in Christ's name, as his disciple. Do you believe this?

›› THE GIFT OF HEALING

We've come to think of healing as absent unless
    it is miraculous.
Unless there is a sun spinning or
    an incurable disease cured,
    healing is dismissed.

The acts of love that heal broken lives
   are overlooked or taken for granted.
Are doctors the only healers in the modern world?
Are priests the only ones whose forgiveness
   is balm for a weary soul?
You, child of God,
   you are the healer God wants to work through.
It is through your eyes that another's dejection will be seen,
   through your ears that another's lament will be heard.
It is your voice that can soothe a tormented heart
   and your touch that is healing ointment for open wounds.
You, disciple of Christ,
   you are the healer God wants to work through.

›› Mind, Body, Spirit

Over the last two decades, scientific studies have revealed what people of faith knew all along: Those with a deep spiritual life and an active prayer life heal faster and stay healthier. Studies are proving that prayer can be a powerful healer; that therapeutic touch lowers blood pressure; that kindness and attentive listening diminish stress.

What about you? Do you need scientific proof to believe that you are a healer? Have you ever seen a person move from tears to calm after you listened to them or affirmed their need? Have you ever put your arm around a person filled with grief or stress and felt their body relax? Have you ever forgiven someone who was terrified of losing your love and witnessed the pure joy that it brings? Do you need proof of your power to heal others, or is the fact you have been healed by others proof enough? We were created to be whole persons, mind, body, and spirit. Go, do your part.

›› Reflection/Journal Writing

Write about your own experiences of being healed by others in body, mind, or spirit. What was that like? What did they do? Do you believe God was acting through that person? Have you ever been the one who healed? How do you know? Did you call upon God in that moment? Have you ever missed an opportunity to heal? How did that feel, when you realized it? Write about what it means to you to be called to heal.

_____

_____

_____

_____

_____

_____

›› ACTION
Look at the very next person you meet through the eyes of Christ. What brokenness do you see? Are they lonely, sad, physically ailing or frail, angry, alienated? Whatever the need, you can offer healing through your words, touch, acceptance, and guidance. Start with the next person you meet, but continue with others after that.

›› CLOSING PRAYER
Jesus, you heal with the sound of your voice and the touch of your hand. You heal because you love. Help me to use the gift of healing that is mine from baptism. Help me to anoint others with love so that they and I may become whole. Amen.

Step Eight on the Disciple's Path: Do Not Be Afraid

›› Introduction

Fear can cripple you. It can hold you back from engaging fully in life. In the life of the spirit, fear can keep you from living on purpose. As you end this forty-day journey in faith and renewal, you may be faced with fear of the unknown expectations of discipleship. Listen to the assuring words of Jesus, "do not be afraid, for I am with you always." Hold on to that message and move forward in confidence.

›› Scripture

Why are you afraid, you of little faith? Matthew 8:26

So have no fear…nothing is covered up that will not be uncovered, and nothing secret that will not become known. Matthew 10:26

Do not fear, only believe. Luke 8:50

>> REFLECTION

Throughout the New Testament, we see Jesus and those who followed him dealing with their fears and overcoming them with the help of God's grace and one another. Mary and Joseph feared for their lives and the lives of their child but had the wisdom to follow the angel's direction. Jesus feared his death and prayed for courage in the midst of his friends. Peter feared the hostility of the Jews and denied Christ. Then he feared his betrayal would be too much to forgive. The early Church lived in fear of persecution and death and the blood of martyrs confirmed that their fear was justified. Yet they met in small groups to share a meal, to pray, to support one another and to offer courage.

The Church exists today because those who feared believed that God's power is greater than all others; they sought and found support for their belief and they did what God placed on their hearts to do, in spite of their fear. You are called to do the same and your reward will be as great.

>> IRRATIONAL FEAR

Fear, itself, is not the problem.
A healthy sense of caution and fear
    can save your life.
Irrational fear distorts life:
    it is unjustified by the facts;
    it is a feeling gone haywire.
People with agoraphobia understand irrational fear.
They look at others going about their business and
    are terrified to go outside and interact.
Others won't use a plane or car or swim or speak in public.
Trapped in their fear,
    they lose life, friends, inner peace—
    opportunities to proclaim the good news
        of God's presence and power.

>> Coping with Fear

What is your worst fear about being a faithful disciple of Christ, about living your life on purpose with God as your priority? Draw or sculpt what your fear of discipleship looks like.

>> Reflection/Journal Writing

As you look at your drawing or sculpture, write about your fears, especially those that keep you from being the child of God you wish to be. Describe what holds you back. Is it rational or irrational? Are there others with whom you could bond that would support you in breaking out of your fear? What could you do for Christ if your fear was not active against it?

_____

_____

_____

_____

_____

_____

>> Action

Choose one thing that you fear about discipleship and do one action in spite of that fear. Perhaps you fear speaking about Christ to another. Today, find someone you know who will be sympathetic to hearing about Christ and weave your testimony into the conversation, as simply as saying, "God led me to talk with you today, and I am so glad." Defeating our fears doesn't have to be spectacular, it is, like all else, a process of small steps.

>> Closing Prayer

Creator, Son and Holy Spirit, fill my life with calm assurance. Banish my fears and show me the path to peace. Amen.

day 40

New Life in Christ

›› INTRODUCTION

This is the day the Lord has made! It marks the end of a forty-day journey of self-reflection and spiritual renewal. It celebrates your decision to change from habits that withered or stagnated your soul to habits that allow you to live on purpose, stretching and expanding your soul's capacity to meet God and to live as a disciple of Christ. Congratulations! It's a day to sing Alleluia, and to rejoice in the fact that you have allowed God's power to work within you and to raise you up to a new life in Christ.

›› SCRIPTURE

Mary! JOHN 20:16

Peace be with you. As the Father has sent me, so I send you…receive the Holy Spirit. JOHN 20:21–22

Blessed are those who have not seen but have believed. JOHN 20:29

›› REFLECTION

Today's readings are taken from the gospel stories surrounding the resurrection of Jesus. They are words spoken by Jesus to those who were trying to understand what had happened to him after they found the tomb empty. Jesus spoke first to Mary of Magdala, then to the fearful disciples, hiding from the Jews, and then to Thomas, who doubted that Jesus had truly risen.

Notice how things proceed. He calls Mary by name and it is in hearing her name called by the Lord that she recognizes him and believes that he is alive and with her. He banishes her fear, giving her what she needs to believe and to commit her life to his way. The apostles he addresses with peace, quelling their fears, showing them the signs that will embolden them for the years ahead and leaving them the Holy Spirit. Jesus patiently overlooks Thomas's lack of faith and proves that fear blinds one to God's living presence. When Thomas demonstrated his belief, Jesus taught the apostles that others would come whose faith would be blessed precisely because it would be "without seeing."

You are among those blessed who have believed and who have been rewarded with seeing the Lord in your midst and recognizing him. You moved past your initial fear of committing to these forty days. You stayed focused even when you may not have seen the way clearly. You took actions that may have been difficult for you and you followed the disciple's path to this day, the first day of the rest of your life.

›› Signs and Blessings

You began eager
> To meet the Lord and
> Follow his way.

You made a covenant
> An agreement to
> Walk with the Lord for
> Forty days.

You persevered in the desert
> Losing your way
> Wondering what would happen
> Seeking and finding healing

Hearing and responding to the call
Ridding yourself of obstacles and doubts.
You have seen the Lord.
Jesus has called your name
Shown you the wounds in your life
Blessed you with the brightness of his glory
Sent you
To tell the others.

>> Spiritual Sight

For some, seeing is believing. It is both true and false for the disciple. Spiritual sight does not look with physical eyes for signs of God's presence and love, though such signs may be present. Spiritual sight looks with the heart, with the spirit, with faith. "Blessed are those who have not seen, but have believed."

If the only things you believe in are what you know through your senses, your life is dull and bereft of glory. Can you touch the love of a mother for her child, or hear the words of comfort in a birdsong? Can you taste the richness of God's mercy or smell the graciousness of God's presence? All can be perceived and understood in the soul of one who believes.

>> Reflection/Journal Writing

As you complete this covenant journey, write about the new life Christ has given you. What rocks have been rolled away from your tomb? When throughout these days did you most hear your name spoken by God? What fears have been allayed by Christ's presence? What doubts have been overcome by meeting Christ anew? Who is this new you? Where and to whom are you being sent?

_____

_____

_____

_____

›› Action

Over the past several weeks you have taken actions in both the realm of self-awareness and in service to others. Now it is time to make a commitment to a life of service.

My Commitment to Live as a Disciple

Lord, I've spent forty days reflecting, praying, and striving to walk the path of discipleship. You've shown me more clearly who I am. You've helped me to cleanse myself of those attitudes, feelings, and behaviors that keep me from living my life more deeply and on purpose. You've listened to my needs and my hopes. You've blessed me with renewed friendships, greater inner peace, deeper prayer, and a desire to serve you in the needs of others.

I want to offer myself humbly, and with a full heart. As I've listened to your voice it has become clear that where I need to commit myself in service is in this way(s):

_____

_____

_____

_____

Lord Jesus, help me keep my commitment and continue to meet you along the way.

Signed _____

Date _____

›› Closing Prayer

Risen Lord, thank you for the gift of new life these days with you have given me. Be with me as I walk the path you've set before me. Pour energy and enthusiasm into every step I take in your service. Amen.